HOLOCAUST

WRITTEN BY
ANGELA GLUCK WOOD

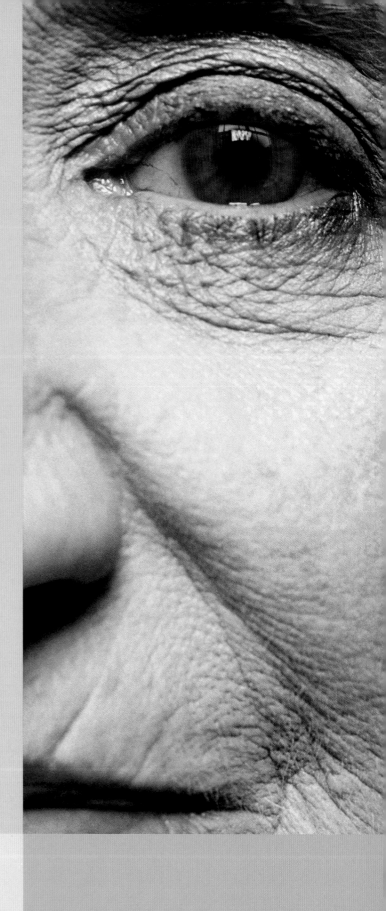

To Ryan
for memory and hope

Consultant Professor Dan Stone
Senior editors Francesca Baines, Claire Nottage
Senior art editors Owen Peyton Jones, Sarah Ponder
Editors Jenny Finch, Fran Jones, Andrea Mills,
Zahavit Shalev, Clare Zinkin
Art editor Marilou Prokopiou
Designers Jim Green, Spencer Holbrook,
Samantha Richiardi, Smiljka Surla, Jacqui Swan, Nihal Yesil
Managing editor Linda Esposito
Managing art editor Diane Thistlethwaite
Publishing manager Andrew Macintyre
Category publisher Laura Buller
Picture researchers Julia Harris-Voss, Kate Lockley,
Jo Walton, Debra Weatherley
Cartographer Ed Merritt
DTP designers Siu Chan, Andy Hilliard
Jacket editor Mariza O'Keeffe
Jacket design manager Sophia Tampakopoulos-Turner
Production controller Angela Graef
DVD project manager Anthony Pearson

First published in Great Britain in 2007 by
Dorling Kindersley Limited, 80 Strand,
London WC2R 0RL

2 4 6 8 10 9 7 5 3 1

Copyright © 2007 Dorling Kindersley Limited, London
A Penguin Company

Quotes taken from testimonies from the USC Shoah Foundation
Institute for Visual History and Education

A CIP catalogue record for this book is available from the British Library.

ISBN: 978-1-4053-1330-8

Colour reproduction by Colourscan, Singapore
Printed by Hung Hing, China

Discover more at www.dk.com

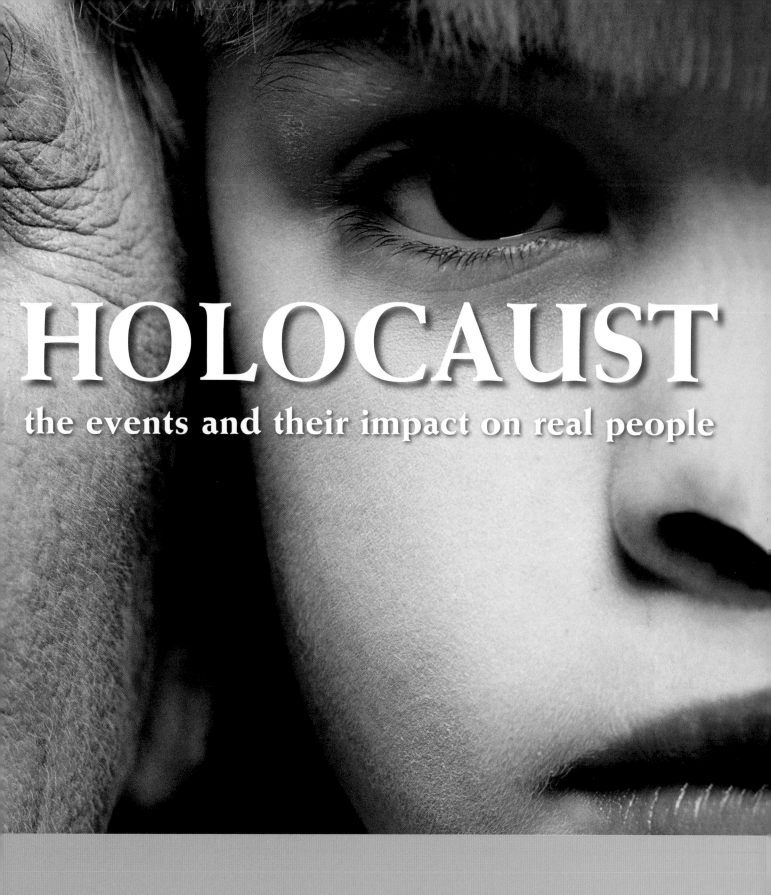

HOLOCAUST

the events and their impact on real people

WRITTEN BY
ANGELA GLUCK WOOD

CLINGING TO LIFE

THE END OF THE WAR

THE AFTERMATH

CONTENTS

The mission of the USC Shoah Foundation Institute for Visual History and Education is to overcome prejudice, intolerance, and bigotry – and the suffering they cause – through the educational use of the Institute's visual history testimonies. With nearly 52,000 video testimonies of Holocaust survivors and other witnesses, collected in 32 languages and from 56 countries, one of the Institute's primary goals is to provide the broadest possible access to these testimonies to people around the world. Throughout the pages of this book, and on the accompanying DVD, you will find first-person accounts of Holocaust survivors and other witnesses taken from the Institute's archive.

This symbol appears throughout the book after some of the quotations of the survivors and witnesses, indicating that the DVD contains testimony clips from that particular person.

*T*HE BOOK YOU ARE HOLDING *in your hands is unique. While it is an authoritative history of the Holocaust that combines text and images in an altogether uncommon way, it is also a human record of the Shoah and its meaning. The pages that follow are replete with statistics and facts, many of them nothing short of horrifying. But these pages also contain the faces and the words of men and women who survived the murderous anti-Semitic world of Nazi-dominated Europe.*

You will also find another singular feature packaged along with this volume, a DVD containing video interviews of many of the survivors whose names are contained in these pages. These men and women spoke of their experiences directly and candidly to the cameras and microphones of the USC Shoah Foundation Institute for Visual History and Education.

The work of the Institute — which was originally called Survivors of the Shoah Visual History Foundation — is the most important professional work of my life. I am deeply proud of its accomplishments and truly thrilled that you will have the opportunity to learn about the Holocaust through the group of testimonies assembled for this book and the accompanying DVD.

Steven Spielberg

FOREWORD
BY STEVEN SPIELBERG

THE JEWS OF EUROPE

FOR MORE THAN 2,000 YEARS Jews have lived in small communities in societies throughout Europe, but it was only from the late 18th century that they were able to play a bigger role in society. The centre of the Jewish community has always been the synagogue, and even non-practising Jews still feel very much part of the Jewish community and its story.

The Passover ceremony
Jewish family life has always been important. Each spring, families celebrate together the festival of Passover to remember the time when their ancestors were slaves in Egypt, but God set them free. This 15th-century illustration shows the special Passover meal (Seder) during which Jews tell stories, sing songs, and remember and retell the experience of escaping slavery.

Beginning of the Golden Age of Spain, with freedom of religion under Muslim rule

The printing press is invented in Germany by Johannes Gutenberg

After the Romans destroy the Temple in Jerusalem, Jews are forced to leave Judea to live in communities throughout Europe and the world

Christianity becomes the official religion of the Roman Empire

North African Muslims conquer Spain

Between 1347 and 1353 the "Black Death" (bubonic plague) kills a third of the population of Europe

EUROPE

c. 33 70 100 c. 400 622 c. 700 c. 900 1099 1271 1347 1450 1453

WORLD

The beginning of the Christian Church

Buddhism spreads to China from the Indian subcontinent

Rise of Islam, spreading from the Arabian Peninsula

Christian Crusaders capture Jerusalem, and kill thousands of Muslims and Jews

Constantinople (now Istanbul), the capital of the Eastern Roman Empire, falls to the Turks

The Italian explorer Marco Polo reaches China

The beginnings of the
Protestant Reformation
of the Catholic Church

The Unification of Germany –
the northern and southern states
join to form a German Empire

First Zionist
Congress held in
Switzerland

In a royal edict, Jews
and Muslims are
expelled from Spain

The French Revolution
sees the end of the rule of
the monarchy in France

The map of Europe
is redrawn at the
Congress of Vienna

The Dreyfus
Affair exposes anti-
Semitism in France

Adolf Hitler becomes
chancellor of Germany

| 1492 | 1517 | 1518 | 1620 | 1789 | 1791 | 1815 | 1871 | 1894 | 1897 | 1914 | 1917 | 1933 | 1939 |

Europeans transport the first
African slaves to the
West Indies

Russian Jews are forced to live in
a restricted area, known as the
"Pale of Settlement"

World War I begins
(to 1918)

World War II
begins (to 1945)

Italian sailor Christopher Columbus leads
a Spanish expedition and reaches the land
mass later named "America"

English religious dissenters
set sail in the *Mayflower* for
Virginia in America

The Russian Revolution sees the
czar abdicate and the Bolsheviks
(communists) take over

THE ORIGINS OF THE JEWS

ALTHOUGH THE ORIGINS OF THE JEWS lie in the Middle East, today there are Jewish communities in many countries, with the largest numbers in Israel, North America, and Europe. Over the centuries, Jews in Europe were driven out of the lands they had settled many times and forced to seek a new homeland. This led to the description of the "wandering Jew".

In the Land of Israel

The Jewish people began as slaves in Egypt, about 3,000 years ago until, they believe, God freed them and promised them their own land, which they called Israel. In their capital, Jerusalem, they built the Temple, as a centre for worship and charitable work. In Jerusalem today there is a large walk-around model of the ancient city, showing the beauty of the Temple.

Deportation to Babylonia

About 2,500 years ago the Babylonians invaded Jerusalem, destroyed the Temple, and carried off the educated and skilled Jews. Centuries later, when Babylonia had become Persia, Jews were once again under threat. But the Persian king, Ahasuerus, was married to Esther, a Jewish woman. As this image shows, she pleaded with him to save Jewish lives.

Exile under Roman rule

When the Jews returned from exile, they rebuilt Jerusalem and the Temple, but had to counter many invasions. About 2,000 years ago, the Romans occupied the land. The Jews were overpowered and in 70 CE the second Temple and much of Jerusalem was destroyed. This marble arch in Rome shows Jews being forced to carry the candelabrum that the Romans stole from the Temple.

Jewish movement in Europe

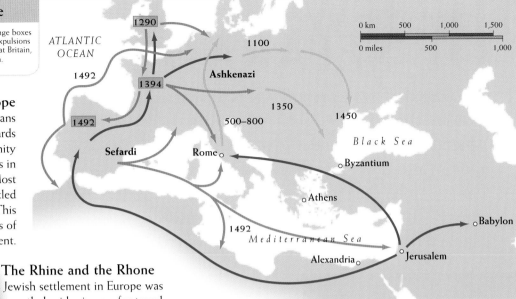

→ Expulsions	Dates within orange boxes mark the major expulsions of Jews from Great Britain, France, and Spain.
→ Dispersal	
→ Migrations	

ATLANTIC OCEAN

1290

1100

1492

1394

Ashkenazi

1492

Sefardi

500–800

1350

1450

Rome

Black Sea

Byzantium

Athens

1492

Mediterranean Sea

Alexandria

Jerusalem

Babylon

The spread of Jews in Europe

When Jerusalem fell to the Romans in 70 CE, some Jews fled towards Babylonia to join the Jewish community there. Others joined communities in northern Africa and then Spain. Most were deported to Rome or settled elsewhere in Europe, as refugees. This map shows the main movements of Jews from that time to the present.

The Rhine and the Rhone

Jewish settlement in Europe was mostly beside rivers – for travel and trade. Communities around the Rhine (Germany) and the Rhone (France) became centres of Jewish culture. This German woodcut shows the lighting of a special lamp for the winter festival of Hanukah.

An invitation and a charter

In 1264, the charter of King Boleslav of Poland granted Jews protection and they were invited to settle as administrators in the area that is now Lithuania, Belarus, and Ukraine. The River Wistula (above) on which they travelled became a symbol of their journeys to and from Poland.

The life of Jews in Spain

Sefardi Jews – those in Spain – enjoyed a Golden Age during Islamic rule. Although never treated as equal to Muslims, they were free to practise Judaism and Jewish culture flourished. Later, under Christian rule, however, most were forced to convert to Christianity or be killed – the rest were expelled in 1492. One family took with them this delicate hand-painted Passover book.

A warm welcome

In 1492, news reached the Ottoman (Turkish) Empire that Jews were banished from Spain. Sultan Beyazit II, shown here, granted Jews safe haven in his Empire and personally greeted them at the port. Most Jews settled and flourished in the European parts of the Empire. Many of the sultans' doctors were Jewish, and it was Jews who set up the first printing presses.

THE JEWS OF SEFARAD

THE HEBREW WORD FOR SPAIN IS *Sefarad*, and Sefardi Jews are those who originated in Spain or Portugal. When the area was under Islamic rule, there were good relations between Jews and Muslims, but under Catholic rule, there was great pressure for Jews to convert. In 1492, both Jews and Muslims were expelled from Spain, and Jews fled to safer countries.

Maimonides

The Jewish scholar Rabbi Moshe ben Maimon is better known as Maimonides. He was born in the 12th century in Cordoba, Spain, where this statue stands. He developed good relations with Muslim scholars and leaders, and was highly respected as a doctor, philosopher, linguist, and specialist in Jewish law.

A secret life

Gracia Mendes was a wealthy Jewish widow living in Portugal during Christian rule. She lived a secret Jewish life while using her money and contacts to help Jews, under pressure to convert to Christianity, to escape. She was hailed as a heroine. This colourful modern image of her is by an American artist.

The Ladino language

When Spanish and Portuguese Jews settled in lands such as Turkey and the Balkans, they continued to speak the same language. This Latin-based language was called "Ladino" and it became the unifying language of Sefardi Jews in Europe. Most Ladino-speaking Jews were murdered in the Holocaust and today very few speak the language. However, there is still interest in Ladino poetry and song.

A broad education

Sefardi Jews value traditional study, and wherever Jews were barred from schools, the Jewish community set up its own. In the late 19th century, the *Alliance Israélite Universelle*, a Jewish organization based in Paris, developed modern schools in several places, including Morocco (above). These schools combined religious education, secular learning, and practical skills.

Sefardi synagogues

In Muslim societies, synagogues resembled the style of mosques in many ways and often used the geometric shapes and swirling patterns of Islamic art. In Christian societies, synagogue art and architecture was more likely to resemble that of churches. This Sefardi synagogue in Florence in Italy, built in 1892, has some of the features of churches of the period as well as the domes and decoration found in mosques.

An estimated 250,000 Jews were expelled from Spain. They were not allowed to take money or valuables.

Sefardi weddings

Many Sefardi Jews, particularly in North Africa, begin wedding celebrations several days before the actual ceremony, with separate parties for the bride and the groom. Here, the female friends and relatives of a Sefardi bride sing and dance in her honour. Parties for the married couple are also held in the week after the wedding.

Ashkenazi Jews in Prague
From the 11th century, many Ashkenazi
Jews settled in Prague, capital of the
Czech Republic. The city became famous
for its traditions of Jewish learning and
hospitality, and became known as "A City
and a Mother in Israel" – Israel meaning
here the Jewish extended family. As this
19th-century painting shows, the clock on
the Jewish town hall in Prague has Hebrew
letters for the hours and runs anti-clockwise,
as Hebrew is read from right to left. The
building on the left is the Altneu Shul,
Europe's oldest functioning synagogue.

THE JEWS
OF ASHKENAZ

ASHKENAZ IS THE OLD HEBREW word for Germany. When
the Jews were expelled from Germany in the Middle Ages,
those that settled in northern, central, and eastern Europe
became known as "Ashkenazi". The language of Ashkenazi
communities was Yiddish. This was based on medieval
German, with some Hebrew expressions, as well as words
from the languages of those places where the Jews settled.

The Golem of Prague
In the 16th century, a series of disasters threatened
the Jewish community of Prague. Ashkenazi
folklore tells how Rabbi Loew created a man-like
creature from clay – known by the Yiddish word
golem – who had the power to save them. This
legend formed the basis for the 1920 German
film, *The Golem* (above).

Rashi of Troyes

The most highly respected Ashkenazi commentator was Rabbi Shlomo Yitzhak, known as Rashi, who lived in Troyes in France during the 11th century. His commentaries on the Bible were influential in his time and continue to be so today. In this monument in Troyes, the Hebrew letters for "Rashi" are carved out and a bright light shines through them. This symbolizes the idea that Rashi's legacy illuminated the name of his hometown throughout the world.

The Jewish community in Germany

From the 4th century, Jews in Germany were valued as merchants who had contacts with communities across Europe. They lived in harmony with non-Jews and were free to practice Judaism. This early woodcut shows a Jewish family rigorously cleaning before the festival of Passover. However, from the 11th century, Christian anti-Judaism led to violence against Jews and communities were driven from city to city. While there was always a Jewish presence in Germany, by the late 15th century, the centre of the Jewish world lay in Eastern Europe.

The Jewish community in Britain

Although there were Jews in England by the 11th century, they were expelled by King Edward I in 1290. However, in 1656, a group of Sefardi Jews from the Netherlands, whose families had fled there from Spain in 1492, were able to settle in England. From 1881 onwards, there was also a wave of Ashkenazi immigration from Russia. Today, British Jews are integrated into British society. This 1920s' photo shows a Jewish boy in London playing at being a bus conductor, complete with ticket punch.

Life in the shtetl
Within the community of the shtetl Jewish law and custom were held in high regard, but towards the end of the 19th century some Jews began to challenge and question this. Marc Chagall (1887–1985) grew up in a shtetl in Russia during this period of change and became famous as an artist after he moved to Paris. Yet his early paintings, such as *Over Vitebsk*, 1914, recall and reflect on shtetl life with affection, and include flying, dream-like characters.

THE WORLD OF THE SHTETL

SHTETL IS THE YIDDISH WORD for a small town or village in Eastern Europe and Russia, or a Jewish section within a town where everyone else was Christian. The world of the shtetl began to disappear in the modern age, and was wiped out by Nazi occupation during the Holocaust. Life in a shtetl was one of poverty and hardship but also one of warm family life, strong community feeling, and deep religious devotion. Many who lived in a shtetl look back on it with great affection.

Pale of Settlement

There was strong feeling against Jews in Russian cities, and so Catherine the Great decided to move them out. In 1791, she created the Pale of Settlement as an area where 90 per cent of Russian Jews were forced to live. There was heavy discrimination – Jews paid double taxes, were forbidden to have higher education or lease land, and suffered violent attacks. Although many tried to leave, the Pale still had more than five million Jews in 1910. The Russian revolution of 1917 brought the Pale to an end.

Pale of Settlement

◾ Pale of Settlement

"Good Sabbath!"

The rhythm of the shtetl week centred round the Jewish Sabbath, from sunset on Friday to sunset on Saturday – a day of rest that begins with the mother lighting candles to spread light and love through the home. The Yiddish greeting *Gut Shabbes!* means "Have a good Sabbath!" This scene from *Fiddler on the Roof* shows a typical Sabbath scene.

The classroom

Heder is Hebrew and Yiddish for "room" but refers specifically to the classroom where Jewish boys – and sometimes girls – received a formal Jewish education, alongside what they learned at home. Going to *heder* involved learning to read Hebrew and studying the Torah and other traditional texts, as these boys are doing.

Street scene

Restrictions placed on Jews meant that most could only work in crafts, such as tailoring, or as traders and peddlers. Often the whole family worked to make a living and in the hope of being able to buy a chicken or fish for the Sabbath. The only place where Jews and Christians would usually meet was the market. This photo from 1916 shows two Jewish men carrying water in a shtetl in Poland.

The role of the synagogue

The hub of a shtetl was the *shul* – the Yiddish word for synagogue, the Jewish community centre. It is a place for daily prayer, for Jewish study, and for social gatherings, such as weddings. Many *shuls* were simple but, when or if a community could afford to, it created an ornate building – like this *shul* in Poland, which was derelict after the Holocaust but has now been restored.

Hasidism

A new movement emerged in Eastern Europe during the 18th century, a new way of being Jewish. It was inspired by the rabbi Baal Schem Tov, nicknamed the *Besht* – Master of the Good Name. He called his followers Hasidim – the pious. He was against dry book learning and in favour of Jews expressing their joy and devotion to God through singing and dancing ecstatically, like these Hasidim.

VOICES
LIFE IN THE SHTETL

For centuries Jews lived across Russia and Eastern Europe in small towns and villages known as shtetls. Although there had been periods of anti-Semitism, for years most Jews had lived peacefully with no illwill from their Christian neighbours. But eventually the anti-Semitism resurfaced and Jews were again subjected to discrimination. Here, people recall their childhood memories.

"WHEN I WAS a young boy, life was very beautiful for us. It was a religious little town and most of the Jews, their whole life revolved around the synagogue. So that means in the morning, early in the morning, when we got up about 4 o'clock or 5 o'clock in the morning we went to heder and from heder we came home and had breakfast and then we went to the normal school, which was with everybody, non-Jews as well as Jews. It was a very, very nice little community. And, after we came back from school, we went back to heder until late in the evening. So that was life when I was a young boy…"

"THE GENTILES USED to wonder at us because we cared so much about religious things – about food and Sabbath and teaching the children Hebrew. They were angry with us for our obstinacy, as they called it, and mocked us and ridiculed the most sacred things. There were wise Gentiles who understood. They were always respectful and openly admired some of our ways. But most of the Gentiles were ignorant. There was one thing, however, the Gentiles always understood, and that was money. They would take any kind of bribe. Peace cost so much a year, in Polotsk. If you did not keep on good terms with your Gentile neighbours, they had a hundred ways of molesting you. If you chased their pigs when they came rooting up your garden, or objected to their children maltreating your children, they might complain against you to the police, stuffing their case with false accusations. If you had not made friends with the police, the case might go to court; and there you lost before the trial was called unless the judge had reason to befriend you."

Mary Antin
(Born in Russia, 1881)
After the assassination of Alexander II in 1881, her family experienced several pogroms in Russia. They eventually settled in the USA.

Peter Hersch
(Born in Czechoslovakia, 1930)
Peter had a happy childhood but later lost all his family apart from his sister in the Holocaust.

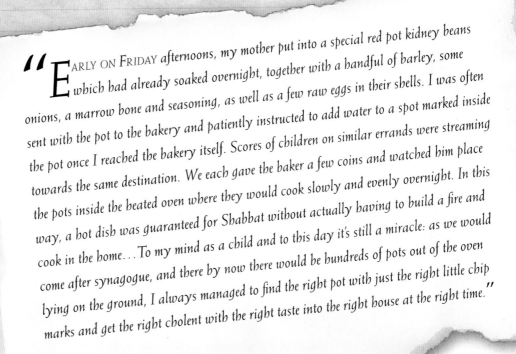

"*Jasionowka was a little town like thousands and thousands of other towns in Eastern Europe in the Pale of Settlement. In Yiddish it was called shtetl and I think it was the Jewish author Shalom Aleihem who described, he said, 'If you want to know what the map of Eastern Europe looked like in the shtetlach,' he says, 'consider a Friday night challah with poppy seeds sprinkled all over.' That's how those towns were sprinkled over Eastern Europe. ....Jasionowka had no electricity, no paved streets. The homes were not much more than huts, many of them with dirt floors, some of them with wooden floors. We had no running water. Water had to be carried from a well, wood had to be chopped and brought in in order to heat and cook with, and life was extremely hard. How in the world my mother managed to raise eight children and keep them all fed and clothed, to this day, I cannot understand it...It was a very wonderful childhood, and I think the security and joy that I took with me from my childhood is really what managed to get me through the Holocaust and the difficult years that followed. I believe if I had not had that strength and that security, I probably would not have survived.*"*

"*Early on Friday afternoons, my mother put into a special red pot kidney beans which had already soaked overnight, together with a handful of barley, some onions, a marrow bone and seasoning, as well as a few raw eggs in their shells. I was often sent with the pot to the bakery and patiently instructed to add water to a spot marked inside the pot once I reached the bakery itself. Scores of children on similar errands were streaming towards the same destination. We each gave the baker a few coins and watched him place the pots inside the heated oven where they would cook slowly and evenly overnight. In this way, a hot dish was guaranteed for Shabbat without actually having to build a fire and cook in the home... To my mind as a child and to this day it's still a miracle: as we would come after synagogue, and there by now there would be hundreds of pots out of the oven lying on the ground, I always managed to find the right pot with just the right little chip marks and get the right cholent with the right taste into the right house at the right time.*"

Bernard Schuster
(Born in Poland, 1928)
Bernard went into hiding during the war and lost many members of his family in the Holocaust.

Hugo Gryn
(Born in Czechoslovakia, 1930)
Hugo's family was sent to Auschwitz, but he and his mother survived. He later became a rabbi.

ENLIGHTENMENT AND EMANCIPATION

The Age of Enlightenment
In the 15th and 16th centuries, Europeans began to question traditional beliefs and challenge Church teachings. Freedom of speech and thought was all. In this painting from 1795, English artist William Blake shows the great scientist Isaac Newton, in the style of religious art, as cosmic designer.

WHEN THE MIDDLE AGES CAME TO AN END, there was a new mood in Europe. Advances in science and technology changed people's lives, and voyages of discovery made Europeans aware of other cultures in various parts of the world. People looked back on earlier centuries as the Dark Ages and believed that they were now in a time of enlightenment and emancipation, when so many possibilities lay before them.

The French Revolution
The slogan on this banner from the French Revolution in 1789, reads "Liberty, fraternity, and equality – or death". This refers to the time when the king and the aristocrats were overthrown and France became the first republic in Europe. It was based on the "rights of man and of the citizen".

Positive portrayal
This 1779 play by Gotthold Ephraim Lessing, a German Christian, explores religious tolerance, and questions whether anyone can know the truth with absolute certainty. The main character is Jewish and is portrayed in a positive way, which was extremely rare in European literature, art, and drama. Lessing probably based *Nathan the Wise* on Moses Mendelsohn, a Jewish friend.

Reform Judaism
The Dohany Street synagogue in Budapest, Hungary, is typical of the style of Neolog or Reform synagogues. It is grand, confident, and modern for its time. Reform Judaism began in Germany in 1800 as a way of helping modern Jews to be both modern and traditional in the way that they practised Judaism. It did this by concentrating on what were essential Jewish beliefs and values.

Emancipation of Europe

☐ Emancipation before 1800
☐ Emancipation between 1800 and 1850
☐ Emancipation between 1850 and 1900
■ Emancipation after 1900

Political emancipation

Following the French Revolution, every Jew in France was given equality with other French citizens, as long as they promised to be loyal to the State and the Jewish community did not expect to be recognized as different from any other. The Edict of Tolerance in Germany made similar promises. Gradually, Jews across Europe were given political emancipation – the freedom to be a full citizen.

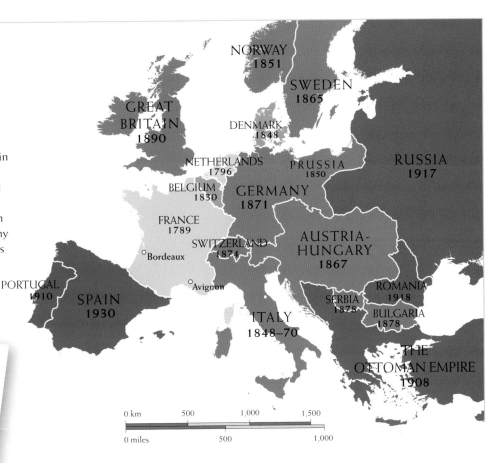

NORWAY 1851
SWEDEN 1865
GREAT BRITAIN 1890
DENMARK 1848
NETHERLANDS 1796
PRUSSIA 1850
RUSSIA 1917
BELGIUM 1830
GERMANY 1871
FRANCE 1789
SWITZERLAND 1874
○ Bordeaux
AUSTRIA-HUNGARY 1867
○ Avignon
PORTUGAL 1910
SPAIN 1930
ROMANIA 1918
SERBIA 1878
BULGARIA 1878
ITALY 1848–70
THE OTTOMAN EMPIRE 1908

0 km 500 1,000 1,500
0 miles 500 1,000

The dream of Zion

Because Jews still experienced prejudice in everyday life, some felt that they could only be equal and free in their ancient homeland, Zion – another name for Jerusalem or Israel. Pioneering Zionists, like these men and women, made their way to the homeland from 1881 onwards. They worked hard at fulfilling the ancient dream to "make the desert bloom".

Land and language

This modern Israeli stamp bears the image of Ben Yehudah, the father of modern Hebrew. Born in Lithuania in the 19th century, he and his wife emigrated to Palestine in 1881. Believing that a nation living in its own land should speak its own language, he revived spoken Hebrew and introduced modern words.

ISRAEL إسرائيل
ישראל 250

Enlightenment in Eastern Europe

By the late 19th century, enlightenment ideas of Western Europe had reached Eastern Europe and Russia, influencing the *baskalah* – the Jewish enlightenment movement. Secular education for Jews was now possible and was considered a great benefit. An important centre of *baskalah* was Odessa, Russia, where this family lived – reading a Russian newspaper would never have happened before the *baskalah*.

JEWISH LIFE IN EUROPE

IN THE MIDDLE AGES, European leaders allowed Jews to settle in their lands, and even encouraged Jewish settlers when they needed their skills. A few worked at the courts of nobles as musicians, diplomats, or interpreters. Towards the end of the 18th century, many European countries began to abolish laws that discriminated against Jews, a period known as the Emancipation, and Jews were able to take part in more aspects of European society.

Jews in the Middle Ages
The medieval Church did not allow Jews to own land or follow some occupations. It also forbade Christians to lend money with interest, but not to borrow money. So Christians used Jews as moneylenders, as this 15th-century German woodcut shows.

In the 1930s there were almost 10 million Jews in Europe.

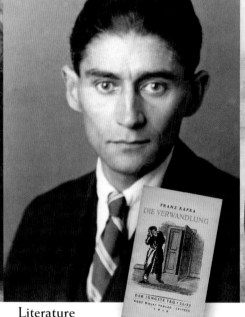

Jews in trade and industry
In the modern age, Jews were able to move into bigger business. Some became familiar household names. Michael Marks (1859–1907) was a poor Russian emigrant to England who started as a peddler, went on to have a market stall, and gradually built up the large chain of stores now known as "Marks & Spencer". Today the Marks family has large charitable trusts.

Literature
Jews are often called "The People of the Book", because they have always valued language, from study of the Torah to humour, poetry, and storytelling. One important Jewish novelist was Franz Kafka (1883–1924), a Czech author, who wrote about people who are confused by life. His most famous work is called *Metamorphosis*.

Science and medicine
In medieval Europe, Jews made up one per cent of the population, yet 50 per cent of doctors were Jewish. Today, many Jews work in medicine and other areas of science. Many have been awarded the Nobel Prize for science, including German-born Albert Einstein (1879–1955). It was Einstein who established the International Rescue Committee to aid victims of Nazism in 1933.

Jewish population in Europe 1933

- ⬛ 1,000,000 and over
- ⬛ 500,000–999,999
- ⬛ 100,000–499,000
- ⬛ 10,000–99,999
- ⬜ 0–9,999

NORWAY 1,500
SWEDEN 6,500
FINLAND 1,800
ESTONIA 5,000
IRELAND 3,600
GREAT BRITAIN 300,000
DENMARK 6,000
LATVIA 95,000
DANZIG 9,200
LITHUANIA 155,000
NETHERLANDS 160,000
GERMANY 565,000
POLAND 3,000,000
SOVIET UNION 3,020,000
BELGIUM 60,000
LUXEMBOURG 2,200
FRANCE 225,000
CZECHOSLOVAKIA 357,000
SWITZERLAND 18,000
AUSTRIA 250,000
HUNGARY 445,000
ROMANIA 760,000
PORTUGAL 1,000
SPAIN 4,000
ITALY 48,000
YUGOSLAVIA 70,000
BULGARIA 50,000
EUROPEAN TURKEY 56,000
ALBANIA 200
GREECE 100,000

0 km 500 1,000 1,500
0 miles 500 1,000

Jewish settlement
Throughout the Middle Ages, Jewish people moved to escape outbursts of violence, or were expelled from one land to another. In modern times, too, some Jews have moved to places of greater safety or better opportunities. In 1933, most Jews lived in Eastern Europe, especially Poland and the Soviet Union (now Russia). These were communities of some of the most traditional and religiously observant Jews in Europe.

Music and drama
Music has always played a large part in Jewish culture. Since the 1800s, there have been many Jewish composers and musicians, including Polish-born pianist Arthur Rubinstein (1887–1982). There have also been reknowned Jewish actors, directors, and producers of film and theatre.

The arts
Traditionally, Jewish art was limited to creating objects used in worship and illustrating texts, but never depicted people. Modern Jewish artists, however, have portrayed people in both sculpture and painting, like this figure by Italian Amedeo Modigliani (1884–1920).

Psychoanalysis
Sigmund Freud (1856–1939), an Austrian Jew, has been called "the father of psychoanalysis", because of his revolutionary work in the study of the mind. In this work, he explored a patient's feelings and behaviour by interpreting their dreams and use of language.

Politics
Once no longer banned from public life, many Jews became involved in politics. Rosa Luxemburg (1870–1919) was one of the most famous Jewish women in politics. A leader of the Polish social democratic movement, she supported the use of strikes to achieve social change.

23

Ecclesia and Synagoga
This window, from the 13th-century church at Marburg in Germany, reveals the early belief that Christianity was superior to Judaism. Christianity represented by Ecclesia, is on the left and Judaism or Synagoga, on the right. While Ecclesia wears crown, Synagoga is blindfolded, refusing to see truth, and holds goat horns, symbol of the devil

Malicious rumours about Jews
For centuries European folklore demonized Jews, portraying them with horns and fork tails, or as reptiles. However, the charge that caused the greatest fear was the "blood libel shown in this medieval woodcut. This was the claim that Jews killed Christian babies for their blood, to make special bread.

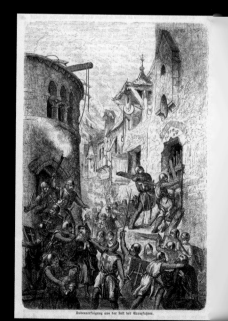

The Crusades
In 1096, the Pope called on Christians to reclaim the Holy Land from Islamic control and Crusaders set off across Europe, fired

THE HISTORY OF ANTI-SEMITISM

ANTI-SEMITISM, THE HATRED OF JEWS, dates from ancient times but was strengthened by the medieval Church, which taught that Jews were to blame for the death of Christ. Along with Christian beliefs came folk ideas of Jews as evil. Although now seen for what they are, both traditions have influenced people and politics today.

Pogroms

The word pogrom comes from the Russian for "devastation" and is the name for the organized massacres of Jews that took place in Russia and Eastern Europe from the 17th century. As recently as 1905, about 3,000 Jews were murdered in some 600 pogroms. This father runs from his burning shtetl with his child.

A Jewish conspiracy

The *Protocols of the Elders of Zion* is a book claiming to contain notes of meetings between Jewish leaders plotting to conquer and control the world, as this cover shows. Although a hoax, it is still published today by anti-Semitic groups. This is a French edition from the 1890s.

The Dreyfus Affair

In 1894, Alfred Dreyfus, a Jewish officer in the French army, was arrested for spying. This poster calls Dreyfus a traitor, yet there was no real evidence against him. Despite this, the trial continued and Dreyfus was found guilty. The case caused a political scandal, and exposed anti-Semitism in France. Eventually the verdict against Dreyfus was overturned.

Theodor Herzl and Zionism

Herzl was an Austro-Hungarian reporter covering the Dreyfus trial. Shocked by the open anti-Semitism of the court, and in France, he concluded that Jews could never be free in Europe and needed a land of their own – the idea of Zionism. In 1896, Herzl organized the first Zionist Congress, to make plans for a Jewish homeland.

Modern anti-Semitism

While there is less anti-Semitism today than in the Middle Ages, or during the Holocaust, it has not disappeared. Lies are still spoken and written about Jews and as a result Jews may suffer discrimination. There is vandalism in Jewish places, such as the desecration of this cemetery, which took place in Herrlisheim, France, in 2004.

"I advise that the Jews' houses also be razed and destroyed. For they pursue in them the same aims as in their synagogues. Instead they might be lodged under a roof or in a barn, like the gypsies. This will bring home to them that they are not masters in our country, as they boast, but that they are living in exile and in captivity, as they incessantly wail and lament about us before God."

Martin Luther, The Jews and Their Lies, *1543*

Jews burnt at the stake, *Nuremberg Chronicle* 1493

NAZI RULE

NAZI RULE BEGAN IN **1933** when Adolf Hitler became leader of Germany, and signalled the end of 12 years of democracy. German laws now became a way of putting the Nazis' racist ideas into practice. Germany aimed to bring all of Europe and eventually all the world under its control. It was a time of terror for non-Nazis, especially those that the Nazis thought were sub-human.

The German Parliament hails the Führer
On 12 March 1938, German forces occupied Austria and annexed it to Germany. The next day, Hitler – known as the Führer, or supreme leader of Germany – convened the German parliament, the *Reichstag*. The members gave him a standing ovation and made the Nazi salute, to show their pride in what Germany had done.

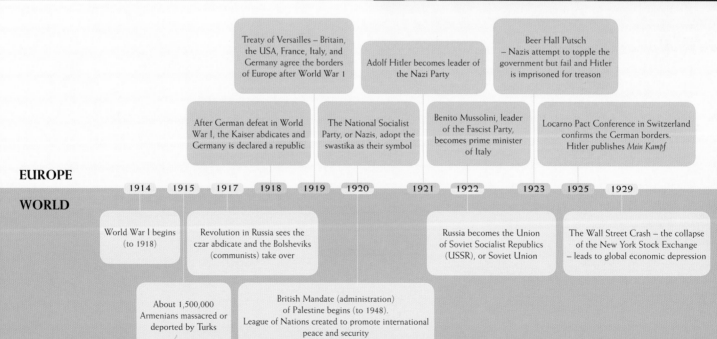

Treaty of Versailles – Britain, the USA, France, Italy, and Germany agree the borders of Europe after World War 1

Adolf Hitler becomes leader of the Nazi Party

Beer Hall Putsch – Nazis attempt to topple the government but fail and Hitler is imprisoned for treason

After German defeat in World War I, the Kaiser abdicates and Germany is declared a republic

The National Socialist Party, or Nazis, adopt the swastika as their symbol

Benito Mussolini, leader of the Fascist Party, becomes prime minister of Italy

Locarno Pact Conference in Switzerland confirms the German borders. Hitler publishes *Mein Kampf*

EUROPE

1914 1915 1917 1918 1919 1920 1921 1922 1923 1925 1929

WORLD

World War I begins (to 1918)

Revolution in Russia sees the czar abdicate and the Bolsheviks (communists) take over

Russia becomes the Union of Soviet Socialist Republics (USSR), or Soviet Union

The Wall Street Crash – the collapse of the New York Stock Exchange – leads to global economic depression

About 1,500,000 Armenians massacred or deported by Turks

British Mandate (administration) of Palestine begins (to 1948). League of Nations created to promote international peace and security

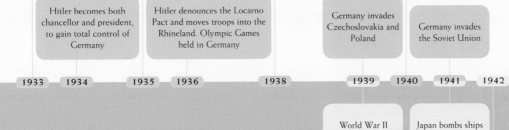

Hitler becomes Chancellor of Germany. Dachau concentration camp set up in Germany to hold political prisoners

In Germany, the Nuremberg Laws outlaw marriage between Jewish and non-Jewish Germans

German troops first move into Austria and then invade the Sudetenland. In Germany, many Jews are killed or wounded in the violence of *Kristallnacht*

The Blitz begins. German planes bomb London and other British cities

Hitler becomes both chancellor and president, to gain total control of Germany

Hitler denounces the Locarno Pact and moves troops into the Rhineland. Olympic Games held in Germany

Germany invades Czechoslovakia and Poland

Germany invades the Soviet Union

1933   1934   1935   1936   1938   1939   1940   1941   1942

World War II begins (to 1945)

Japan bombs ships in Pearl Harbor, Hawaii, USA

The USA enters World War II

29

THE LEGACY OF THE GREAT WAR

WORLD WAR I (1914–18) became known as The Great War because of its vast scale, its huge impact on nations and individuals, and the extensive damage. Germany suffered heavy casualties, lost land, and had to pay reparations (compensation). This left the economy weak and the people low in spirits. The Nazis gained support by blaming the Jews for the losses and persuading Germans that they would make Germany great again.

"Jew Count"
Christian images on German cards showed the Church's support for the war. Despite Nazi claims that Jews had shirked military service a "Jew Count" in 1916 showed that a high proportion of Jews had volunteered. More than 100,000 served in the army and 35,000 were decorated for bravery.

THE FORGOTTEN MASSACRES

During World War I the Ottoman (Turkish) Empire fought on Germany's side – and most Turks were Muslim. The Turks accused their Armenian Christian minority of siding with Russia, their enemy. As a result, it is claimed that in 1915 the Turks massacred 1,500,000 Armenian Christians. Turkey disputes this figure and claims that the Armenians simply died in the way of war. This poster (right) was part of an American campaign to provide relief for the surviving Armenian Christians forced to flee Turkey. Hitler is reported to have used the Armenian massacres to justify his own policies, saying that as no one remembered the Armenian genocide, no one would care how the Nazis dealt with the "Jewish problem".

Armenian Christians find refuge aboard a French ship

Germany loses The Great War
The region of Lorraine, which Germany and France both claimed as their own, became a battlefield in World War I. These German soldiers, who had once proudly marched off to war, hopeful of victory, have been captured by the French in the Lorraine region. Their faces reveal their sense of national shame.

Treaty of Versailles

The war was ended by the Treaty of Versailles, a peace treaty created by the Allies – Britain, France, Italy, and the USA – and signed in 1919, near Paris. The Allies wanted to ensure that Germany could never go to war again and it had to agree to reduce its armies, lose land, and pay crippling reparations. This cartoon expresses Germany's deep sense of humiliation.

The Locarno Pact

In 1925, Britain, France, Italy, Germany, Belgium, Poland, and Czechoslovakia met in Locarno, in Switzerland, to confirm the borders of Europe as agreed in the Treaty of Versailles. But the question mark on this election poster of 1928 shows there was a feeling it need not be respected. By 1936 Hitler had gone back on the Locarno Pact completely.

During World War I, more than 12,000 German-Jewish soldiers were killed on the battlefield.

SETTING THE STAGE

HITLER KNEW the German people were depressed by their losses in World War I and used their disillusionment for his own aims by blaming "outsiders", meaning communists and Jews. This united the Germans against a common enemy. Hitler also wanted to disrupt meetings of political opponents and protect himself from attacks, so he formed a private army of storm troopers, also known as Brownshirts.

Anti-Semitism

The Nazis played on the fears of ordinary Germans by depicting Jews as controlling, greedy, and cruel. In this poster from 1924, the Star of David identifies the giant wire-puller as Jewish. He is controlling the workers, pulling the strings as if they were his puppets.

Anti-communism

The Nazis also sought to discredit the Social Democratic Party (SPD) which had voted against Nazi laws in 1933. This poster shows an SPD angel, wearing the hammer and sickle symbol of communism, walking hand in hand with a wealthy, capitalist Jew, warning Germans that neither could be trusted.

Hyperinflation

After World War I, the German economy was weak and the cost of living was high. By 1923, inflation – continual increases in prices – was at a staggering rate. Printing more money just made it worthless. Many Germans burned money for heating because it was cheaper than buying fuel. A new currency was introduced in 1924.

Italian Fascism

In 1922, the Fascist Party, under Mussolini, came to power in Italy, emphasizing national unity, military values, and hatred of communism. In this poster, storm troopers hold a picture of Hitler and point to the Italian flag to show Hitler's attraction to Fascism.

In the 1928 elections, fewer than three per cent of Germans voted for the Nazi party.

Political speeches

Hitler was drawn to the German Workers' Party, but suggested changing the name to the National Socialist German Workers Party – the *Nationalsozialistishe Deutsche Arbeiterpartei* or Nazis. Although socialism stressed equality, Hitler added "national" to mean that only Germans were equal. He was often invited to give political speeches because of his power to stir up people's hatred, and is depicted here addressing the crowd in a beer hall.

The Munich Beer Hall Putsch

In 1923, Hitler decided on a putsch, a sudden and illegal use of force, to overthrow the government. Armed storm troopers led by Hitler burst into a government meeting. Hitler fired shots in the air and declared the start of the National Revolution. Other Nazi leaders seized the war ministry, arresting Jews and political opponents. The next day Hitler and 3,000 Nazi supporters marched through Munich before police stopped them.

MY STRUGGLE

After the Nazi march in Munich, Hitler was captured and charged with high treason. Although he was found guilty, he received the minimum sentence of five years in prison. There he began writing his ideas about the evils of Jews and communists, the connections between them, and what could be done. These ideas were published in 1925 in Hitler's book *Mein Kampf* (My Struggle). Five million copies were published by 1939. Millions more have been published since and the book has been translated into many languages.

POPULAR SUPPORT

AT FIRST THERE WAS LITTLE SUPPORT for the Nazis in Germany, but they learned the powerful appeal of uniforms, symbols, rallies, and salutes from the experience of the Italian Fascists. Nazi theories of race also helped to make ordinary Germans feel superior and strengthened popular support. Gradually the Nazis increased their appeal, especially with young people.

Children and young people
The Nazis used youth movements to influence Germans at an impressionable age, and joining a youth movement became almost compulsory. Children wore uniforms and took part in activities that emphasized discipline and fitness, with tests of endurance and self-sacrifice. This girl is collecting money for youth hostels and homes.

Theories of race
Posters like this were hung on German classroom walls as an aid to education. The Nazis drew on 19th-century theories that people could be divided into separate races, some superior and some inferior. The "master races" were the Northern Europeans, especially the Germans, who they claimed were descended from Aryans, the first people of ancient India.

The Hitler salute
The Nazi salute was a sign of loyalty to Hitler. It was modelled on the salute of the Italian Fascists, the ancient Romans, as well as the ancient Germans. It showed a war-like spirit, with the arm resembling a raised spear. Nazi supporters would salute and greet each other, and at mass gatherings like this youth rally, would proclaim *"Sieg Heil"* meaning "Victory and Hail".

The Nazi flag
Hitler designed the Nazi flag. He chose red, black, and white, the historical colours of Germany's flag, as a sign that democracy and the Weimar Republic were over. Red stood for the social idea of Nazism, white for nationalism, and the black swastika for the struggle of the Aryan man. At this 1933 rally in Nuremberg, members of the SS carry the flags as standards.

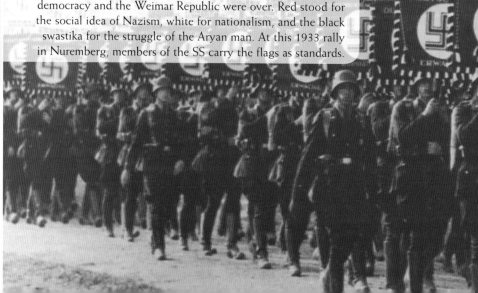

Es lebe Deutschland!

In 1938, Hitler was Time *magazine's man of the year.*

Eine schlägt auch für uns

In 1920, the Nazis adopted the symbol of the hooked cross, an ancient German symbol for the god of thunder. It was similar to the swastika, an Indian sign of goodness, which was appropriate as the Aryan race originated in India. The swastika appeared in Nazi insignia and even on everyday items, such as this clock.

The cult of Hitler

In this poster, Hitler is depicted in the same way that Jesus is often portrayed at his baptism – with a powerful spiritual light in the sky and a dove hovering overhead. This was typical of the growing cult in which Hitler was treated as a god. Many Germans believed that he had supernatural powers, and some addressed prayers to him if they were worried or unhappy. This poster declares "Long live Germany!"

IN BY THE BACK DOOR

HITLER'S ACCURATE PREDICTION of the Great Depression that began in America in 1929, led people to believe he could help Germany's economy. The Nazis then used the trebling of German unemployment in 1930 to win support for their plans for a confident, independent Germany. However, not everyone was convinced, so Hitler resorted to other methods to gain total power.

Election campaigner during the German presidential election, 1932

Wall Street Crash
In 1929, when New York stockbrokers in the Wall Street Stock Exchange called in loans, the value of stocks fell. In panic, Americans cashed their bank accounts and the Stock Exchange collapsed. The German and American economies were closely linked, so Germans were also affected.

DATE	NAZI SHARE OF VOTES	DEPUTIES ELECTED	VOTES IN MILLIONS
20 May 1928	2.6%	12	0.81
14 September 1930	18.3%	107	6.41
31 July 1932	37.3%	230	13.75
6 November 1932	33.1%	196	11.74
5 March 1933	43.9%	288	17.28

Nazi election victories
The Nazis were slow to win votes and get deputies elected to the government, as the chart above shows. In fact, in 1932 support dipped. The Nazis never won an outright majority, even in 1933 when they came to power.

Hitler becomes chancellor
After the 1932 elections, president Paul von Hindenburg refused Hitler's request to be made chancellor, afraid that Hitler would be dictatorial. But in January 1933, the Conservative parties supported Hitler, hoping to use him to their advantage. The president finally agreed. Hitler immediately took over all the functions of state, making Germany a dictatorship. To increase popular support, Hitler organized huge rallies, like this torchlight procession in Berlin.

The burning of parliament
As Hitler could not be certain that he would win an election, he used other means to achieve his aims. As he hoped, horrified crowds gathered when the parliament building, the *Reichstag*, mysteriously caught fire. A communist caught with matches was forced to confess. As a result, Hitler was able to adopt emergency powers to ban socialists and communists from the elections.

PERIODS OF GERMAN GOVERNMENT

The First Reich: The Holy Roman Empire	843–1806
The Second Reich: The German Empire	1871–1919
The Weimar Republic: A democratic government	1919–33
The Third Reich	1933–45

One People, One Empire, One Leader
Inspired by Mussolini's title *il Duce* – the Duke, Hitler took the title of *der Führer* – the Leader. He expected to be addressed as *Mein Führer*, My Leader. This propaganda poster declares "One People, One Empire, One Leader", a slogan that aimed to make Hitler an icon of unity.

The beginning of the Third Reich
Hitler wanted to make laws without the interference of parliament, so he proposed the Enabling Act. Storm troopers outside the parliament building ensured the law was passed. Hitler now had a legal right to be a dictator. When the president died in 1934 Hitler became both chancellor and president – he had gained total control.

THE AUTOBAHNS

Hitler dreamed of a German superhighway network that would be the best in the world, and a milestone in the building up of the German people. Here, in September 1933, he is seen ceremonially digging the foundation of an *Autobahn*, or motorway. Good roads were a great advantage to the German people and increased Hitler's popularity. They had symbolic value as a sign of German achievement and collective effort. They also signalled that all Germans were connected, quite literally, and so the country was united.

Ein Volk, ein Reich, ein Führer!

"I had been skating that day … when I got home …
we heard that Hitler had become Chancellor.
Everybody shook. As kids of ten we shook."

Leslie Frankel recalls hearing the news that Hitler had become Chancellor of Germany

The Nazi parade of the flags at the Victory Party in Nuremberg, Germany, September 1933

VOICES
NAZI GERMANY

When Hitler came to power in 1933, nobody could have foreseen the horrors that lay ahead, even though people were alarmed at the increasing climate of anti-Semitism in Germany. However, many Jews decided not to flee because they did not want to leave their homes and thought the situation would pass.

" *IN 1935, WHEN Hitler was already very much in control and had become Chancellor, I went to Cologne to meet some of my old university friends. Then I went to Berlin and went to see the woman in charge of the Jewish community. She gave me the information that I wanted and before I went, the sight of all those flags, the blood red flag, you know, with the swastika, struck terror, really terror into me. And you never knew when you'd be picked up! I was very scared on the train, especially at the borders. But fortunately I got through and then, as I sat with this woman, she said, 'You're an American, you can get out of here, we can't, no country wants us. You can get out. Go out. Go out and scream! Scream so the whole world will know what we're suffering here. Just get out.' So I left and I went to Poland.*"

Ruth Gruber
(Born in Germany, 1911)
Ruth left Germany before the war to live in the United States. She recalls a return visit in 1935.

"*I* WENT TO Germany to look up some of our old friends and families and the stories I heard all over Germany from the Jewish people – were just terrible. It wasn't even as bad as it was in later years, but everybody was concerned about what was happening. A lot of people wanted to get out of Germany, but they said, 'Well, my mother's here and my father's here and they're old and we don't want to leave them. We have our business here and we don't want to leave our business.' I suggested to many of them that it was a good time to leave Germany because, as an outsider, I had a better picture of what was going on. What disturbed me most is that Germany was in the midst of rearming! Everything was in armament. Every person was in uniform. Tanks were on the streets and there were parades and loudspeakers…and everybody was singing Deutschland Über Alles and Heute Deutschland Morgen die Welt, you know, Today Germany, Tomorrow the World, and there was a strange spirit of nationalism. And of course the situation for the Jews was getting worse, although a lot felt that the problem was temporary and would eventually go away. It didn't go away, as we all know, and I left Germany. I have a note from a series of talks I gave after I came home in which I said, 'There is absolutely no future for any Jews in Germany. I think the Jews have to get out of there.' But nobody was listening.*"*

"*T*HE REAL SERIOUS change that I noticed was when we found one morning, when we went to school, that all the other children had formed two lines in front of the school house door and as we walked through those two lines they beat us up! I went to the teacher and I complained and he said, 'Well, what did you expect you dirty Jew?' And from that we figured that he had the children every morning in church (they had to go for mass every morning) and we figured that what he had done is organized the children to beat us up.*"* 🔘

Emma Mogilensky
(Born in Germany, 1923)
Emma was just fifteen years old when she experienced the anti-Semitism she describes here.

Fred Baer
(Born in Germany, 1910)
Fred's family went to the United States before the war started. He recalls the reluctance of the Jews to leave.

THE THIRD REICH

HITLER'S REGIME was called the Third Reich – or Third Empire. It began as a police state but increasingly controlled people's actions and thoughts. The *Schutzstaffel*, or SS, started in the 1920s as Hitler's personal guards but, after 1933, it became a second army. The Secret State Police, the Gestapo, also had great power and tortured people who had been arrested without charge.

Hitler the icon

By the time of the Third Reich, there were more pictures of Hitler than of anyone else in history. The idea was to fill people's minds with his image, and in some pictures Hitler appears as a religious or folk icon. This famous painting from 1938, by Austrian artist Hubert Lanzinger, is called *The Flag Bearer* and portrays Hitler as a knight.

Dachau concentration camp

Dachau was one of the first concentration camps in Germany, dating from 1933. It held 1,200 inmates, mostly political prisoners. Conditions were not as harsh as in later camps, but many died from the poor conditions or were killed for breaking a camp rule.

The Nuremberg Laws

With the Third Reich in power, relationships between Jews and non-Jews were often mocked in public. Some people were made to wear placards saying that they were a "Jewish pig" or were marrying a "Jewish pig". In 1935, anti-Semitism was legalized in two Nuremberg Laws. One made marriage between Jews and non-Jews illegal to protect German "racial purity" and the other stated that only "pure" Germans were Reich citizens.

North Sea

DENMARK

Baltic Sea

FREE CITY OF DANZIG

MEMEL

LITHUANIA

NETHERLANDS

Hamburg

GERMANY (EAST PRUSSIA)

BELGIUM

Berlin

POLAND

Warsaw

LUXEMBOURG

GERMANY

Breslau

0 km	100	200	300
0 miles	100		200

FRANCE

Nuremberg

SUDETENLAND
(incorporated into Third Reich, September 1938)

Prague

CZECHOSLOVAKIA

Stuttgart

LIECHTENSTEIN

Munich

Vienna

SWITZERLAND

AUSTRIA
(incorporated into Third Reich, March 1938)

ITALY

HUNGARY

YUGOSLAVIA

Land-grabbing

Hitler was determined to make Germany a great power again that could dominate Europe. *Lebensraum*, meaning "living space", was a Nazi term for land-grabbing. As this map shows, this began with Austria in 1938. Hitler planned to unite all German-speakers in one country and create a "Greater Germany", which would expand eastwards.

Into Austria

Hitler urged Austrian Nazis to demand that Austria and Germany be united. Then, in March 1938, the German army invaded Austria. This parade in Innsbruck was held the next day, after the Austrian troops were sworn into the Third Reich. The *Anschluss* (political union) was complete.

The Sudetenland

The *Anschluss* strengthened Germany's drive for more land. German speakers in the Sudetenland, a region of Czechoslovakia, wanted to join Greater Germany and Hitler claimed that, by invading the Sudetenland, he was freeing them. As the troops marched in, locals had to salute. Then in 1939 Hitler invaded Czechoslovakia from the Sudetenland.

43

NAZI PROPAGANDA

IN HIS BOOK *MEIN KAMPF*, Hitler wrote that the use of emotion, rather than reason, would convince people to share Nazi beliefs. The Minister for Propaganda, Joseph Goebbels, promoted Nazi ideals in an emotional way to influence people's thoughts. Everything the Third Reich communicated had a political message, from speeches and posters to films and architecture.

Nazi "heroes"

The Nazis wanted people to perceive them as heroes, able to attack evil and protect Germany from harm. In this poster, the Nazi figure is depicted as a brave warrior. Many propaganda posters adapted imagery from Christian legends and European folklore.

Art and architecture

Hitler banned, hid, or destroyed modern art because he believed it was corrupt. Instead, he promoted great painters of the past and commissioned new work in traditional styles. The architect Albert Speer rewarded Hitler's friendship by designing imposing buildings, such as this grandstand at the Nazi Party rally grounds in Nuremberg.

Hitler as saviour

To record the 1934 Nazi Party Congress, Hitler commissioned a propaganda film called *Triumph of the Will*. Its theme was the return of Germany as a great power and Hitler as a German saviour bringing the nation glory. The film director, Leni Riefenstahl, used clever techniques, such as this shot placing Hitler in line with the church but in the foreground so that he appears to tower over it.

Within days of becoming chancellor, Hitler closed down the printing presses of all organizations that opposed him.

Children, church, kitchen

The ideals that the Nazis glorified for women were *Kinder, Kirche, Küche*, which means children, church, kitchen. Family images such as this were meant to motivate women to strive for these goals. White, non-Jewish women were encouraged to have large families in order to produce soldiers and workers, and expand the Aryan population.

Selective breeding

This poster claims that "God cannot want the sick and ailing to reproduce". It aimed to persuade people that sterilization was necessary to prevent the birth of babies with illnesses or disabilities. In later years, sterilization would be replaced by the outright killing of "undesirables", including races that the Nazis believed were inferior.

Forbidden friendships

During the 1920s in Germany there were about 250,000 black people as well as other minority groups, such as Jews and Romanies. The Nazis claimed that all these people were *Untermenschen*, or sub-humans, and polluted the country. This photograph depicts a friendship between a white, non-Jewish woman and a black woman. The relationship is discouraged with the caption "A loss of racial pride".

Victimized groups

In this Nazi filmstrip, links are made between stereotyped images of "sub-humans", including Arabs, Asians, and Africans. Joining these people and shown very large is a stereotypical Jew. By visually connecting these demonized groups, the Nazi belief that they are guilty people is reinforced in the minds of their target audience – white, non-Jewish Germans. The caption on this poster reads "The Jew is a bastard".

THE RISE OF ANTI-SEMITISM

JEWS LIVED in permanent fear during the Nazi period. Law after law was passed to deprive them of their rights and restrict their lives. Most non-Jewish Germans turned against the Jews living in their local communities, and violent outbursts were frequent. However, a large proportion of German Jews did not leave the country because they believed the situation would not last and Germany was their home.

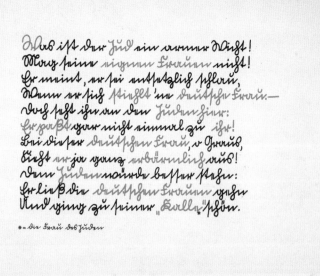

Burning books
Just as the Nazis destroyed any art that they considered to be immoral or "un-German", they also burned books – many of them by Jewish authors. Bonfires such as this one near the Berlin Opera House were a spectacle for the public to watch, and reinforced hatred of the writers.

Public humiliations
Nazis attacked and humiliated Jews in many ways, such as by pulling hair from men's beards or forcing them to dance in public. Jews were also made to scrub the streets, as shown here in Vienna, while Austrian Nazis and local residents watched.

"Night of Broken Glass"
On 9 November 1938, Joseph Goebbels, Hitler's Propaganda Minister, organized attacks on Jews in Germany, Sudetenland, and Austria. Known as *Kristallnacht* (Night of Broken Glass), 96 Jews died and hundreds were wounded. More than 1,000 synagogues and 7,500 Jewish businesses were destroyed. Jews had to pay huge sums to repair the damage and 30,000 of them were sent to concentration camps.

Stereotypes of Jews

German children were shown anti-Semitic ideas and images from an early age. The Jew as a kidnapper in this storybook played on their fears. Other stereotypes of Jews were as money-grabbing cheats, monsters, and slimy creepy-crawlies. In time, the images themselves became codes for "Jew".

In 1938, 18,000 German Jews were expelled from Germany overnight.

"J" for Jew

This passport belonged to a young Jewish woman called Edith Baum. Every Jew had to have their passport clearly stamped with the letter "J". On passports and other documents, Jewish men had to add the name "Israel" and Jewish women the name "Sarah". These additions were aimed at making it impossible for Jews to hide their identity.

Assimilated German Jews

In the 19th century, Germany became a safe and comfortable place for Jews and many had prospered, feeling fully integrated. Some stopped practising their religion and some converted to Christianity. This German Jewish family looks like any other German family, but it was assimilated Jews such as these that the Nazis found most worrying.

Revival of old fears

The popular Nazi newspaper *Der Stürmer* often published anti-Semitic articles. This 1934 edition promoted the idea of a Jewish conspiracy by showing Jews faking their loyalty to Germany. The paper also featured stories about a religious ritual that Jews had been falsely charged with centuries before, that of draining the blood of Christians.

Anti-Semitic laws

Between 1933 and 1939, German Jews lost almost all of their civil rights and were singled out for persecution. Eventually, in Germany and Nazi-occupied regions, Jews were forced to show on their clothing that they were Jewish. In some places this was with a Star of David badge, in others an armband.

1933

Jews no longer allowed to work as lawyers, judges, or civil servants. Jewish children forbidden from playing with other children.

1935

Jewish writers, musicians, and art dealers forbidden from working. Jews only allowed to sit on public benches marked "For Jews".

1936

Jews had to hand over their bicycles and typewriters. Jewish vets forced to stop working. Jewish converts to Christianity classed as Jewish.

1938

Jewish doctors and midwives forced to stop working. Jews no longer allowed to have their own businesses. Jews forbidden to attend the cinema, theatre, opera, concerts, or swimming pools. Jewish children expelled from German schools.

1939

Jews forced to hand over their valuables to the police. Jews evicted from their homes without reason or notice. Jews not allowed out after 8pm in the winter and 9pm in the summer.

A synagogue on fire in Bielefeld, Germany, during the Night of Broken Glass, November 9, 1938

"While I was travelling to Dinslaken I heard in the train that anti-Semitic riots had broken out everywhere, and that many Jews had been arrested. Synagogues everywhere are burning."

Yitzhak S. Herz recalls the terror of Kristallnacht while he was working at Dinslaken orphanage.

VOICES
JEWS UNDER THE NAZIS

The Nazis introduced many laws to discriminate against Jews and deprive them of their rights. Then, on *Kristallnacht*, 9–10 November 1938, synagogues and Jewish businesses were destroyed by soldiers and ordinary citizens. Later, Jews were forced to carry identification – in the form of new ID cards – and also to wear a yellow star on their clothes, marking them out as Jewish.

"WE SAW THEM starting to march on the streets, and of course the next day, all the stores already had signs saying, 'Juden sind hier unerwunscht' ('Jews are not wanted here'). And the Jewish stores, you know, 'Jude', they wrote on them and all kinds of things happened. There was a lot of things going on and you were sitting there and you didn't really know what is going to happen – and soon we found out. It was terrible. The first thing that I remember very well, when I came home from school, (this was just in the beginning), I went on the street where we lived and there was a whole bunch of people standing around shouting and shouting, 'Juden!' and so on and so forth, and here I see my mother on the street, on her feet, cleaning the street! They took her to clean up the signs that they put on the streets for the election. And I said, 'Ma! What are you doing here?' And she said, 'Thea, go home! Go home!' She didn't want me to stay there. And I cried tremendously and I didn't go home, I stayed there saying, 'Mummy, mummy!' And the people, they had no compassion whatsoever. They were full of hate. All of them. All of them."

"IN THE WINTER they came and picked up my father and mother, and then us too, to shovel the snow. We had to shovel snow for hours. And the people were standing around laughing. I remember I had a pair of boots and they wanted them... They didn't take them but I was afraid I would have to go barefoot in the snow."

Thea Rumstein
(Born in Austria, 1928)
Thea recalls some early anti-Semitic attacks on her family before they were all deported to Theresienstadt ghetto.

"THERE WAS A big table there in the entry of the City Hall and people that I used to see on the street, that I knew, were there and signing us up because we had to have new identification cards. Everyone in Europe always had, and in France always had, like we have here, a social security card or a driver's licence as an identification card. We just had an identification card with where you live, where you were born, if you were a student or working, or whatever. And then on that same card they changed it and they gave it another colour. Instead of being beige like before, it was a yellow one and across was a stamp, and it said 'Juif' on it, 'Jew', and it was like you brand an animal – that's how I felt."

"I WAS SO upset! I can't tell you. I went over to my girlfriend who we sat together in the school years and the mother opened the door and she said, 'I heard you were a bloody pig, a Jewish pig. Don't come here again!' and threw the door in my face. I stood there like an ox! I couldn't understand what had happened! My best girlfriend's mother, she looked after me as if I was her child – from one day to the other she changed."

"ON NOVEMBER 10TH 1938, in the morning, we went out to school and suddenly we saw smoke and fire and temples. They had started a pogrom in Berlin and started breaking windows. They broke the windows of all the Jewish stores and took the merchandise. They brought big, big picket signs that said, 'Don't buy from the Jews!' and they started burning the synagogues."

Michelle Cohen-Rodriguez
(Born in France, 1935)
Michelle recalls the degradation she felt when forced to carry a Jewish identification card.

Sigi Hart
(Born in Germany, 1925)
Sigi recalls *Kristallnacht* in 1938, when Jewish shops and synagogues were smashed and burned.

Leonie Hilton
(Born in Germany, 1916)
Leonie relates her shock and dismay when her best friend's mother no longer accepted her.

VICTIMS OF NAZISM

THE NAZIS BELIEVED a wide range of people were inferior to them and had no place in Germany or even the world. They believed in the survival of the fittest, with the strong having rights over the weak. In particular, the Nazis wanted to destroy two groups who would neither change or be "cured" – the Jews and the Romanies. Though often called "gypsies", Romanies found this name an insult.

Targeting Romanies

Living a traditional nomadic (moving around with no fixed home) existence, about 30,000 Romanies lived in Greater Germany and 1,000,000 in Eastern Europe, mainly in Romania and the Soviet Union. The Nazis built on a long history of prejudice against Romanies in Europe. They measured their faces, claiming that Romanies, like Jews, were a different race – "life unworthy of life".

About 220,000–500,000 Romanies were killed during the Holocaust.

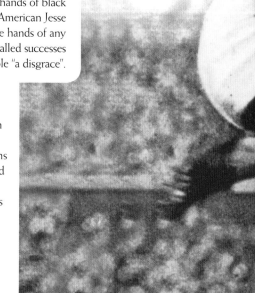

Prejudice against blacks

There were few black people in Germany, and Nazi hatred of them emerged when Germany hosted the Olympic Games in 1936. To avoid shaking the hands of black people who had won medals, such as American Jesse Owens, shown here, Hitler did not shake the hands of any winners. Propaganda Minister Goebbels called successes by black people "a disgrace".

The Germanization of Poles

The Nazis thought the Poles were sub-human and also wanted their land. Although the Nazis persecuted the Poles and killed millions of them, they thought some Polish babies and children "looked" German. They kidnapped about 50,000 of them, including these babies in baskets, to be adopted by German parents and "Germanized".

Political opponents

The Nazis would not tolerate opposition, whatever the "race" of the opponents. They banned other political parties and rooted out their members, especially communists because they believed that they conspired with Jews to rule the world. This photograph, taken secretly in 1933, shows one location where political opponents were imprisoned, tortured, and forced into hard labour.

Homosexuals

The Nazis thought that homosexuals were inferior because they would not have children and continue the race. They also believed that homosexual males were not real men. Fearing that homosexuality would spread as a social disease, the Nazis shut down homosexual clubs and bars, such as this one in Berlin in 1933.

People with disabilities

Nazi plans for the perfect race were threatened by the mentally ill and physically disabled, so at least 300,000 people were sterilized in 1934 to stop them having children. Hereditary health cards like this one were created to track any family history of disability.

Jehovah's Witnesses

Due to their faith, Jehovah's Witnesses do not support a government or carry weapons, so they did not support the Third Reich. By 1935, it was illegal to be a Jehovah's Witness and many were taken to camps. Jehovah's Witness Johannes Steyer painted Hitler as a "saint" to show how most Germans saw him.

WORLD WAR II

THE WORLD WATCHED THE RISE of Nazi Germany but did nothing. In 1938, Hitler made his first moves to dominate Europe and when German troops invaded Poland in 1939, war was declared. The war between the Allies (Britain, the Soviet Union, the USA, and other countries) and the Axis Powers (Germany, Italy, and Japan) was fought over territory, not the Nazis' brutal treament of minority groups.

The invasion of Czechoslovakia

Hitler threatened to invade Czechoslovakia unless Britain supported his plan to take over Sudetenland, an area of German-speaking Czechoslovakia. In September 1938 in Munich, Britain and France agreed that Germany could have Sudetenland. In return, Germany agreed not to occupy more of Europe. On his return, British Prime Minister Neville Chamberlain held up the Munich Agreement and called it "peace in our time". But in March 1939, Germany seized the rest of Czechoslovakia.

German invasion of Poland

On 1 September 1939, German troops advanced into western Poland and Britain declared war on Germany. Within two weeks, Poland was completely occupied and Germany called some of the territory it captured "The General Government" because some of the occupied Polish land was incorporated directly into Germany. This train is taking German troops to Poland in late September. The handwriting on the side reads, "We are going to Poland to thrash the Jews."

The Blitz

With Britain at war with Germany, there were air raids over London and other cities from August 1940. These raids were nicknamed The Blitz, from the German word *Blitzkrieg* meaning "lightning war". These people are sleeping in one of London's underground stations, which were used as air raid shelters.

The USA enters the war

After the German occupation of France, the USA began debating whether to support Britain in the war. Then, on 7 December 1941, Japan, an ally of Germany, attacked Pearl Harbor in Hawaii, USA. The next day the USA declared war on Japan, and three days later Germany and Italy declared war on the USA. This poster encouraged Americans to buy savings bonds to help fund the war.

BUY WAR BONDS

Areas occupied by the Nazis in 1942

- German occupied
- German allies or occupied by German allies
- Neutral
- Allies

The Nazi occupation of Europe

By 1942, Germany had occupied and was controlling more than half of Europe, as well as part of the Soviet Union.

NORWAY 1940
SWEDEN
FINLAND
IRELAND
GREAT BRITAIN
DENMARK 1940
SOVIET UNION
REICHSKOMMISSARIAT OSTLAND 1941
NETHERLANDS 1940
BELGIUM 1940
GREATER GERMANY
REICHSKOMMISSARIAT UKRAINE 1941
OCCUPIED FRANCE 1941
PROTECTORATE OF BOHEMIA AND MORAVIA 1939
GENERAL GOVERNMENT 1939-1941
SLOVAKIA
SWITZERLAND
VICHY FRANCE
HUNGARY
PORTUGAL
SPAIN
CROATIA
ITALY
MONTENEGRO
SERBIA 1941
ROMANIA
BULGARIA
ALBANIA
GREECE 1941
TURKEY
CYPRUS

0 km 500 1,000 1,500
0 miles 500 1,000

Operation Barbarossa

Germany planned to create a colony within the Soviet Union and invaded in June 1941. Code-named Operation Barbarossa, the invasion involved three million troops and more than 3,000 tanks. The German soldiers and tanks almost reached Moscow, but suffered such heavy casualties that they were eventually forced to surrender.

THE GHETTOS

ALTHOUGH THERE WERE GHETTOS in the Middle Ages to which Jews were restricted, they had all closed down by the beginning of the 19th century. The Nazis revived the idea of the ghettos and used them to confine their victims – mostly Jews, but also Romanies. Conditions in the ghettos were extremely harsh: food and water were scarce, people were crammed together in small spaces, and the constant presence of Nazi troops was very oppressive.

Footbridge in the Łódź ghetto
The sealed ghetto of Łódź, Poland, was divided into two parts. Ghetto residents were not allowed to use the streets and could only cross from one part to the other using the footbridge.

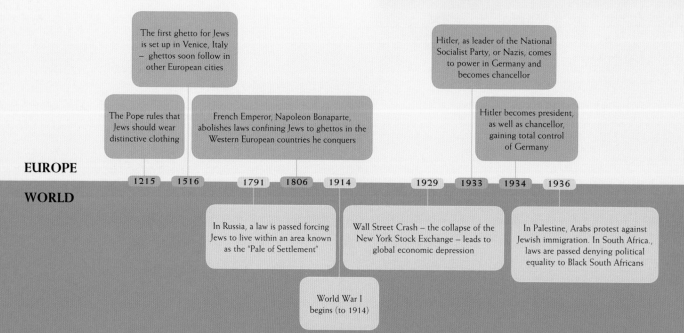

The first ghetto for Jews is set up in Venice, Italy – ghettos soon follow in other European cities

Hitler, as leader of the National Socialist Party, or Nazis, comes to power in Germany and becomes chancellor

The Pope rules that Jews should wear distinctive clothing

French Emperor, Napoleon Bonaparte, abolishes laws confining Jews to ghettos in the Western European countries he conquers

Hitler becomes president, as well as chancellor, gaining total control of Germany

EUROPE

| 1215 | 1516 | 1791 | 1806 | 1914 | 1929 | 1933 | 1934 | 1936 |

WORLD

In Russia, a law is passed forcing Jews to live within an area known as the "Pale of Settlement"

Wall Street Crash – the collapse of the New York Stock Exchange – leads to global economic depression

In Palestine, Arabs protest against Jewish immigration. In South Africa., laws are passed denying political equality to Black South Africans

World War I begins (to 1914)

Germany invades Poland.
Emmanuel Ringelblum begins his
diary in the Warsaw ghetto and
sets up the *Oyneg Shabbes* group

Deportation of Jews to death
camps from ghettos in Poland,
and other areas of German-
occupied Europe, begins

Hitler commits suicide
in his bunker in Berlin,
Germany

Kristallnacht (Night of Broken
Glass) – all over Germany,
Jews and their property are
attacked

Nazis establish a
Jewish ghetto in
Łódź, Poland

Warsaw ghetto
uprising, Poland

The first milk churn of documents
hidden by *Oyneg Shabbes* group is
discovered in Warsaw

1938   1939   1940   1941   1942   1943   1945   1946   1950

World War II
begins (to 1945)

Japan bombs ships
in Pearl Harbor,
Hawaii, USA

The USA drops
atomic bombs on
Hiroshima and
Nagasaki, Japan

In South Africa, laws are passed
enforcing a system of racial
segregation, called apartheid (to 1994)

The USA enters
World War II

THE IDEA OF THE GHETTO

THE IDEA OF SEPARATING Jews from Christians began in the Middle Ages, when bishops or lords organized closed-off areas for Jews. In Venice, the Jewish quarter was established on the site of a metal-casting foundry – or *ghetto* in Italian. In 19th-century Russia, Jews were confined to the Pale of Settlement, a larger and more open area than a ghetto. By the time the Nazis came to power, the ghettos and the Pale had gone, but the Nazis revived the idea of separation.

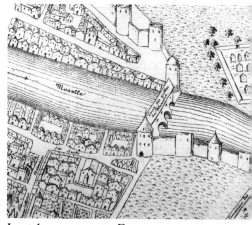

Jewish quarters in Europe
This 16th-century drawing of a Jewish quarter in France shows the high wall separating it from the rest of the town. Living conditions were poor, and inhabitants were cut off from other people. However, they were protected from attacks and allowed to practise their religion and run their own community.

When the Warsaw ghetto was set up, a third of the population of Warsaw was crammed into an area of just 3.4 sq km (1.3 sq miles).

The Pale of Settlement
In 1791, Russia annexed part of Poland and created an area in which to settle 90 per cent of all Russian Jews, known as the Pale of Settlement. Jews could only leave the Pale with special permission, but they could travel within it, for example, to a market like this one. Jews living in the Pale paid double taxes and were forbidden to lease land or receive higher education.

Hats and badges
In 1215, the Pope ruled that Jewish men and women should wear something distinctive. In some places this was a hat, in others a badge. The man on the right is wearing what came to be known as a "Jewish hat".

The Venice ghetto
Following a decree by the Pope, the Venice ghetto was created in 1516. This street, in the area where the ghetto once was, looks very different today from the way it did in the Middle Ages. Streets were extremely narrow and extra storeys were added to the houses to cope with the overcrowding.

Napoleon closes the ghettos
The French Revolution in 1789 led to the emancipation of Jews in France, giving them many of the same rights as other French citizens. From 1806 onwards, Napoleon closed down ghettos in the countries he conquered, and abolished laws restricting where Jews could live.

Nazi creation of ghettos
This model of the Łódź ghetto was created by a Jew who witnessed firsthand its creation by the Nazis in 1940. The Łódź ghetto was the largest after the one in Warsaw. Other ghettos were built along similar lines, though some were open (without walls). When the Nazis invaded Poland in 1939, creating ghettos was a priority as a means of controlling and restricting Jews.

Ghettos beyond Poland
Between 1939 and 1945, the Nazis created hundreds of ghettos in the Soviet Union, the Baltic States, Czechoslovakia, Romania, and Hungary. Increasingly, ghettos came to be used as temporary holding centres prior to deportation.

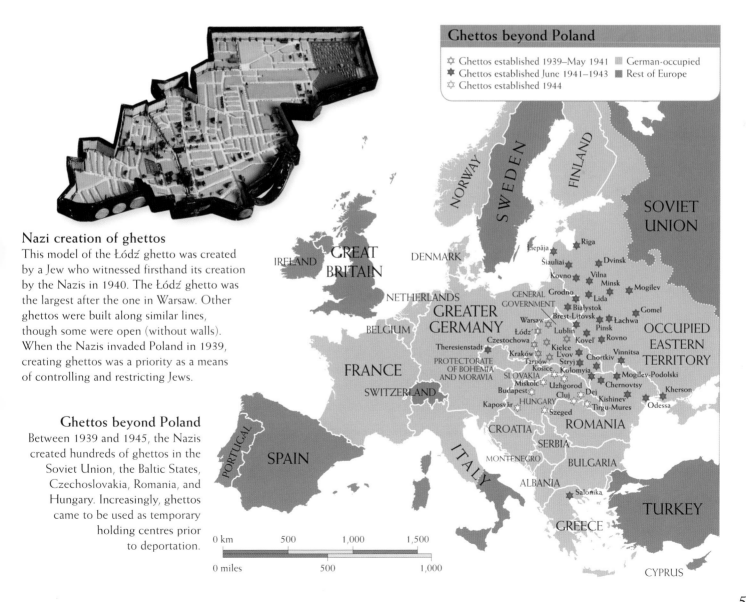

Ghettos beyond Poland
- ✡ Ghettos established 1939–May 1941
- ✮ Ghettos established June 1941–1943
- ✡ Ghettos established 1944
- ▨ German-occupied
- ▨ Rest of Europe

"If our bodies live forever,
they can do so only through
our children ... I would only
like to be conscious when I
die. I want to be able to tell
the children 'Goodbye' and
wish them freedom to
choose their own way."

*Janusz Korczak, who established an
orphanage to help Jewish children whose
parents had been deported or killed*

Mother and baby in the Łódz ghetto. Photograph by Henryk Ross from his book *My Secret Camera*

SUFFERING AND HARDSHIP

SUFFERING AND HARDSHIP IN THE GHETTOS was a deliberate approach taken by the Nazis. The starvation was so bad that the Nazis could lure people into being deported with a promise of something to eat. Although the greatest hardship was starvation, the Nazis committed other atrocities in the ghettos, including many acts of violence.

"Ghetto disease"

Jews in the ghettos called the starvation and exhaustion they experienced every day "Ghetto disease". The Nazis limited the official food intake to a portion of bread, amounting to only 200 calories per person per day. Many people, including children like those above, begged on the streets. People would even sell their clothes and blankets to buy food, but would then freeze when the winter came.

Desperate for food

During the Holocaust, Germans in general received about 93 per cent of the food that they had beforehand, Poles about 66 per cent, and Jews only 20 per cent. Adding to this amount by illegally producing food was a very important, but dangerous, task. In some ghettos, there were plots of land. These young people have been growing food in the Łódź ghetto.

Smuggling
One solution to the food shortage was smuggling. These men are scaling the Warsaw ghetto wall, but most of the smugglers were children, who could squeeze through holes in the walls or even wriggle through sewers. Those who looked Aryan were the most successful, but there was a huge risk of being caught.

Like Jews, the Romanies were considered by the Nazis to be *Untermenschen*, or sub-humans. But, unlike Jews, the Romanies were traditionally a nomadic people, living in scattered and travelling communities, rather than concentrated in towns and cities. The Nazis rounded up many Romanies and brought them to the already overcrowded ghettos. There, like the Jews, they lived in cramped conditions, as in this Romany camp within the Łódź ghetto. Most Romanies were not used to living in cities or to staying in one place, and many of them did not speak Polish, which made everyday life extremely difficult.

"Big Brothers"
The American Jewish Joint Distribution Committee (JDC) relieved suffering in the ghettos, providing services such as this soup kitchen in Warsaw. But it could no longer operate in Europe after the USA entered World War II. In 1943, Polish Jewish leaders wrote to American Jewish leaders asking them to become their "big brothers" and to draw attention to their plight and send money for food and medicine.

Only one per cent of the apartments in the Warsaw ghetto had running water.

Death and disease
Disease was rampant in every ghetto. Most people became sick because there was so little food and it was of such poor quality. There was no heating in the ghettos and people suffered from the bitter cold in winter. They caught infections because of overcrowding and the lack of water to keep clean. This man is already seriously ill, and sights of people dying or dead on the pavements were very common. Well over a million people are known to have died in the ghettos. If all the statistics were available, the figure could be even higher.

GHETTO ORGANIZATIONS

TO CARRY OUT THEIR ORDERS, the Nazis set up *Judenraete* – Jewish councils. A community could elect members of its *Judenrat* only with Nazi approval. The *Judenraete* rightly suspected the Nazis of exploiting them, but usually did not dare disobey orders. Jewish communities expected them to bargain with the Nazis for better conditions, which often made the job of the *Judenraete* a difficult balancing act.

Ghetto money
The Nazis confiscated Jews' money and valuables and, in several ghettos, issued coins and banknotes for use only in that particular ghetto. This ghetto money had no value anywhere else, and Jews called it "Monopoly money". Chaim Rumkowski, leader of the Łódź *Judenrat*, issued currency himself – nicknamed "Rumkies".

Health and welfare
As well as undertaking the functions that the Nazis demanded, *Judenraete* also took on other roles. They organized families to share rooms, took care of orphans, and also set up clinics, like this one. Despite scant resources, many doctors were courageous and creative. Dr Vittorio Sacerdoti in Rome invented a disease he called "K Syndrome", which scared the Nazis and spared 45 Jews from deportation.

Ghetto police
The Nazis ordered the *Judenraete* to create ghetto police forces. They were the first Jewish police forces in Europe, carrying out duties dictated by the Nazis and some that the *Judenraete* decided. They also did whatever seemed necessary in the community. Jewish police were recognizable by their uniform and badge.

Sickness and death
Hospitals were managed by *Judenraete* on very scant resources, and doctors faced moral dilemmas about which patients to feed and treat. Handcarts like this were an increasingly common sight in the ghettos and had a dual function – for taking the sick to hospital and the dead to the cemetery.

Work

In order to make the ghettos useful to the Nazis and so reduce the number of Jews deported, *Judenraete* created as many factories and workshops as they could. These Jews in a clothing factory in the Warsaw ghetto were thought fortunate, despite the long hours, because they got extra food rations.

Food rations

Judenraete were responsible for issuing ration cards like this one, entitling the bearer to perhaps 200–300 calories a day or a loaf of bread to last five days. At times there was not even any food available to buy. *Judenraete* also set up communal kitchens, serving people soup or whatever else might be available.

Mind and body

Schools and orphanages were run by the *Judenraete*. If the Nazis closed them down, they operated in secret. Communal kitchens often doubled as informal schools, where teachers told stories and gave out food. This picture, *Story Hour*, painted by Pavel Fantl (1903–45) in Terezin, shows how education helped people survive in the ghettos.

MY SECRET CAMERA

Sensing that the ghetto would not survive, the Łódź *Judenrat* decided to photograph ghetto life so that their story could one day be told. In secret, several workers took photos of what the Nazis did and made them do. One photographer, Henryk Ross, captured everyday life and personal situations. This picture – one of 3,000 he took – shows two boys playing "cops and robbers", one dressed up as a ghetto policeman. Ross survived the Holocaust and found the negatives he had hidden, some of which were in good condition.

CULTURAL LIFE AND SPIRITUAL RESISTANCE

DESPITE THE HIGH WALLS OF THE GHETTOS and the military strength of the Nazis, many people in the ghettos escaped or fought in their hearts and minds. For most, resistance took the form of clinging to the love of family and friends, holding on to traditions, and strengthening their hope. It was a great tribute to the human spirit that, even though the Nazis tried to dehumanize them, the Jews went to great lengths to preserve their humanity.

Jewish youth movements
Youth groups became even more important after the Nazis closed the schools. They offered young people education or training, involved them in welfare work, and gave them inspiration and hope for the future. Here, members of the Front of the Wilderness Generation in Łódź are enjoying themselves in a circle dance.

Children in the ghettos
Many children's parents died from starvation or disease, or were deported. In Warsaw, Janusz Korczak ran a large orphanage. When the Nazis deported the children to a death camp, he went with them so that they would not be alone. This event is portrayed in this sculpture in the Warsaw Jewish cemetery.

Starving and studying
In Warsaw, ghetto doctors decided that some good should come from the starvation that everyone experienced. They studied the effects of malnutrition on the mind and body, and their very useful research was published after the Holocaust. Here, medical staff, who themselves are starving, are trying to treat a starving patient in hospital.

Crying and laughing
Many people found they could forget their suffering for a while by listening to or performing music, like those in this ghetto orchestra. Jews needed to express their sadness, but also often made jokes about the conditions in the ghetto. Several ghettos had thriving Jewish theatres, which meant a lot to both the actors and the audience. Crying and laughing together was an important way for those in the ghettos to feel that they were still human, whatever their situation.

More than 6,000 drawings and paintings were hidden in the Terezin ghetto during the Holocaust.

"The Führer builds the Jews a Town"
Terezin, which the Nazis called Theresienstadt, was a so-called "model ghetto" in Czechoslovakia. People could get art materials and created many drawings and paintings, like this one by a child, expressing memories of a happier life. But a Nazi propaganda film hugely exaggerated the education and cultural activities that went on and pretended it was a town that Hitler built specially for the Jews.

Praying and praising
Jewish worship continued in the ghettos and was even more intense during the Holocaust, despite (or perhaps because of) the fact that the Nazis forbade it. Many, like this group studying Jewish texts in the Kraków ghetto, made huge sacrifices to practise their religion, running the risk of being caught.

VOICES
LIFE IN THE GHETTOS

Life inside the ghettos was appalling. Overcrowding and unsanitary conditions led to disease, and in the winter people froze to death. There was never enough food, despite the attempts of those who crawled through the ghetto walls, risking their lives to bring back some bread or a few potatoes. People were deported in their thousands, but no one knew for certain where they were taken.

"WE HAD TO go to a pump to get water, which during winter was frozen. It was an existence that is very, very hard to believe. We were there to be used as forced labour. My father was forced to reinforce the fence that surrounded the ghetto and we were given so little food that in three months he died of starvation. Although you can expect it if somebody is ailing, when you see somebody just wither away, you wonder whether in a very short time you will have the same fate. The traumatic thing about my father's passing was the lack of burial. The corpses were placed outside wherever you lived, on the street, and a wagon came by in the morning collecting the people that had died during the night. You saw heaps of bodies."

"THE GHETTO WAS designated quite a few blocks around, cordoned off and they built a high wall, probably about a ten-foot wall, with glass on top of the wall so you could not scale that wall…On the other hand they left a little bit of a hole at the gutter, for the water to run through…It was a very small hole, but enough for me as a little kid to crawl through. I wasn't the only one that was crawling through, other kids would crawl through not knowing what happens on the other side. So you made your way through and I would go out from the ghetto and buy some food. I couldn't carry too much. I would buy one loaf, sometimes some potatoes, a few different things — which were pretty cheap, not to spend too much money, bring it into the ghetto. My father would sell it and we had a little bit of what was left over from that."

Henry Greenblatt
(Born in Poland, 1930)
Henry recalls how he and other children used to escape from the Warsaw ghetto to bring food back.

Henry Oster
(Born in Germany, 1928)
Henry's family were deported in 1941 to the Łódź ghetto in Poland where his father died.

"WHAT CAN I tell you? I can only talk about Terezin and how it stands out if I think about what came afterwards. While we were there it was...there was a constant dying going on. There were epidemics there, people had encephalitis, which is an inflammation of the brain membranes, people had jaundice, which I had too. Don't forget the proximity of people living together — one got it, everybody got it. No medication there or very little. So whoever got well, got well, whoever didn't get well, died. Especially the older people, the older people, they died like flies. What stands out? We were still together...we still wore regular clothes, even though it was old and it was no good, and we had our hair and we looked like human beings. That stands out."

"WE STAYED IN the ghetto for a few weeks and the transportation was going all the time. Trains and trains were leaving and we didn't know where they were going. They were filling up cattle trains. Some of them said they were going to work camps, others said they were going to Poland. Rumours were flying around. Everybody wanted to know where they were taking the trains and so every five minutes you heard something else, 'They're going to nice farms, they're going to work!'. And then, 'No! they're going to horrible places!'. This was unsettling us so much that we couldn't eat, we couldn't sleep — we were worried sick. Families were being separated and neighbours were being taken. It was an awful, awful place."

Thea Rumstein
(Born in Austria, 1928)
Thea describes the terrible living conditions in the Terezin ghetto in occupied Czechoslovakia.

Peter Hersch
(Born in Czechoslovakia, 1930)
Peter recalls his time in the Mukacevo ghetto and the fear caused by the constant deportations.

Adam Czerniakow, Warsaw

As head of the Warsaw *Judenrat*, Czerniakow received the announcement, in July 1942, that the Nazis intended to deport 6,000 Jews each day until none remained. Czerniakow managed to get exemptions for a few, including the girl in this photo, but the Nazis would not spare the children in the Korczak orphanage. The next day, as an act of protest, Czerniakow took his own life.

Yakob Gens, Vilna

The Nazis abolished the Vilna *Judenrat* and put Gens, former head of the ghetto police, in charge. When they demanded victims, he chose the elderly, believing that a productive ghetto would survive. His aim was to ensure that at least some would live, and he explained that if he did not hand over a thousand Jews, the Nazis would take ten thousand. He once said, "May the aged among the Jews forgive us. They were a sacrifice for our Jews and our future."

Chaim Rumkowski, Łódź

Rumkowski – shown here with the Nazi head of the ghetto administration – was nicknamed "King Chaim". He believed that the way to protect most Jews was to give the Nazis whatever they asked for. When deportation calls came, he urged parents to surrender their children.

LIQUIDATION OF THE GHETTOS

EVEN AS THE GHETTOS WERE EMPTIED, it was not always clear to their inhabitants what lay ahead. Jews had varying fantasies and fears about their destinations. Some knew about the death camps and did not resist deportation. Some tried to escape. Others did not know or did not want to know.

Filling and emptying
The gross overcrowding in this room in Poland was typical of ghettos everywhere. Often several families had to share a single room, and personal family conversations or privacy between a husband and wife were impossible. People burnt their furniture for cooking and heating, and had to sleep on the floor – sometimes in shifts.

Saying goodbye
The liquidation of the ghettos separated many families. This mother is being parted from her son. Sometimes children were deported because they were less useful to the Nazis. Parents being deported sometimes hid their children or entrusted them to anyone who could take them.

A farewell letter
Zipporah Berman sent this tender and loving note to her sister, who was already living in Palestine, knowing that she might never see her again. She wrote in Hebrew, which she learned because she also hoped to go and live in the Jewish homeland.

A final wave
From some ghettos, deportations were by train. Here, though, Jews are crowded onto open trucks, meaning the journey may only have been a few hours long. We might wonder who these women are waving to as they are carted off, and whether they know where they are being taken and what will happen to them.

LARGEST GHETTOS	
Warsaw, Poland	400,000–500,000
Łódź, Poland	205,000
Lvov, Ukraine	110,000
Minsk, Belorussia	100,000
Terezin, Czechoslovakia	90,000
Budapest, Hungary	70,000
Chernovtsy, Romania	50,000
Białystok, Poland	35,000–50,000
Riga, Latvia	43,000
Vilna, Lithuania	41,000
Kovno, Lithuania	40,000
Lublin, Poland	34,000

Population figures of the largest ghettos
Within months these large populations of Jews were reduced to just a few thousand, as the Nazis carried out mass deportations.

VOICES
LIQUIDATION OF THE GHETTOS

Although life in the ghettos had been extremely hard, many people had no idea how much worse it was to become. As families were separated and crammed into cattle trucks, fear grew and rumours spread. Conditions were terrible and many people died on the journey before they even arrived at the camps.

"So WE PACKED up what we had and of course all the clothes, and we were taken to the train, to these cattle trains, and put in. It must have been a hundred, a hundred and twenty, we were pushed in, they pushed us like sardines. I remember them pushing us because the wagons were full but they still kept pushing people in. And there were no windows except the little one on top, with wires, I remember that because I had to be lifted up to look if we went through stations, to tell them what kind of a station it is. So the little ones were lifted up. And from there the train went direct from Mukacevo, the train went straight to Auschwitz... We arrived in Auschwitz, I remember it was during the daytime we arrived there... People were crying. People were talking saying, 'Where are they taking us? What are they going to do with us? Will we all be killed?' And others said, 'Don't talk like that!'"

Peter Hersch
(Born in Czechoslovakia, 1930)
Peter and his family were deported to Auschwitz from Mukacevo ghetto in 1944.

"*W*E WENT INTO *wagons and looked around and there was just a little hole on top of the train and we thought, 'Where are we going? Where are we going?' Nobody knew where we were going. But then when they opened up the doors, I mean, this was like three days of agony — there was no food, no bathroom, I don't know where we went, wherever we were we went — and all of a sudden they opened the doors and we saw* 'Arbeit Macht Frei' ['Work Brings Freedom'] *and* 'Oswiecim' ['Auschwitz'] *you know, that was the station. And whenever I see these train things, you know…it's terrible.*"

"*T*HE NEXT DAY *my father said to me, 'I want to talk to you'. He says, 'Always remember that you are a Jew.' He says, 'Whatever happens, remember that and remember your name because I hope we will all survive. But in case you don't see me and you survive, go to Jerusalem because we have a cousin there.' And he made me repeat the cousin's name and address many times. I was nine years old. 'Tell him your name is Silberberg. Tell him who you are and he will take you in'. That was so sad for me. We left together, my aunt and I, and my father and mother. To one side were the tracks, and to the other was the gate where the SS were standing guarding the ghetto. I remember my father turned around and I turned around to look and I wanted so much for my mother to turn around but she didn't, she just walked straight away. That was the last time I ever saw them.*"

Thea Rumstein
(Born in Austria, 1928)
Thea and her mother were deported to Auschwitz, so they could join her father and brother.

Rose Silberberg-Skier
(Born in Poland, 1934)
Rose's parents were deported in 1943 from Srodula ghetto. She went into hiding with her aunt.

THE WARSAW GHETTO UPRISING

THE WARSAW GHETTO UPRISING was one of the most remarkable events of the Holocaust. The Jewish resistance fighters were hugely outnumbered by the Nazis, yet they succeeded in denting Nazi capability and confidence. They inspired the breakout from the Treblinka death camp and an uprising in the rest of Warsaw.

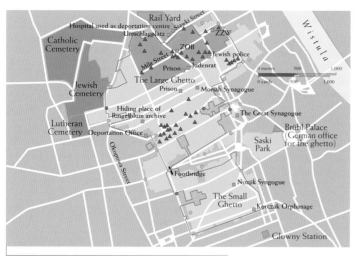

Map Key

- 1943 ghetto at the time of the uprising
- 1940 ghetto
- — Boundary of the ghetto on 22 July 1942 when the deportations began
- ● Entrance to the ghetto in 1940
- ● Entrance to the ghetto in 1942
- ▢ SS Office for valuables taken from Jews
- ▲ Bunkers and fighting points

The largest ghetto
When the Nazis created the Warsaw ghetto in October 1940, some 350,000 Jews lived in the city – about 30 per cent of the population. The ghetto was 20 times more densely populated than the rest of Warsaw and, as this map shows, the Nazis reduced the space even more.

Walls all around
In November 1940, the Nazis enclosed the ghetto by making the Jews build a 3-m (10-ft) high wall around it. They aimed to make it impossible for Jews to reach other parts of Warsaw. Despite this, the Jewish Military Union (ZZW) organized the smuggling of food and weapons.

From Warsaw to…?
In July 1942, the Nazis announced that they would resettle 6,000 Jews per day "in the East". This was alarming, but the Jews did not know exactly what it meant. By September, 300,000 had been transported from this station to a death camp, where most were killed immediately. About 55,000 people were left in the ghetto.

During the Warsaw ghetto uprising, the Germans had 135 machine guns to the Jews' two machine guns, and 1,358 rifles to the Jews' 15 rifles.

The ghetto fights back

In January 1943, during a deportation, members of the Jewish Fighting Organization (ZOB) fired on German troops. The troops retreated after a few days. Although the victory was temporary, it encouraged the fighters. This memorial in Warsaw commemorates their determination.

The ghetto rises in revolt

On 19 April 1943, German troops and police entered the ghetto to deport anyone still there. It was the eve of Passover, the Jewish festival of freedom – and that theme was in the hearts of the 750 Jewish fighters in the ghetto, who were determined to fight to the finish. General Jürgen Stroop, the head of the police, ordered his troops to set the ghetto on fire.

The struggle continues

The fire raged and the fighters were vastly outnumbered by Nazis. Even knowing that they had no chance, they still refused to surrender. Many took to bunkers in the cellars, and some moved from building to building through the sewers. Others were captured amid the rubble.

The revolt is crushed

Having ordered the sewers to be flooded, Stroop finally crushed the revolt on 16 May 1943. Of the 55,000 Jews captured, about 7,000 were shot and the rest deported to death camps. In his report Stroop wrote, "The ghetto is no more." The fighters had held out for three weeks – three weeks longer than Stroop thought his forces would need to overpower them.

THE RINGELBLUM ARCHIVE

IN MANY GHETTOS, Jews felt the need to record their experiences so that the world would know – either then or later – what was happening. The most wide-ranging collection was in Warsaw. The Ringelblum Archive, named after the historian who started the research, is a major source of information about Nazi activities, conditions in the ghettos, and how Jews responded.

Emmanuel Ringelblum
Ringelblum started a diary in 1939, and later used it to record and reflect on ghetto life. He would write for hours in the library (left, in photo), which still stands, though the Great Synagogue next to it was destroyed by the Nazis. When the deportations began, he wanted to reflect a wider range of ghetto experiences and ideas so he urged others to join in his research and creativity.

"Sabbath delight"
The Ringelblum group met in the library on Saturday afternoons and called themselves *Oyneg Shabbes*, meaning "Sabbath delight". They wrote and drew on any scraps of paper they could get. They also collected writings and drawings by children and adults, and examples of community events like the concert advertised in this poster. Ringelblum was extremely proud of the way the group worked together towards a common goal.

"Between life and death"
The *Oyneg Shabbes* group thought that if the free world knew the truth about the ghettos, it might strengthen the fight against Nazism. Seeing it as an act of resistance, they contributed all kinds of material to the archive. Gela Seksztajn, who donated this self-portrait, described herself as "at the boundary between life and death" and urged Jews to do everything to stop the tragedy being repeated.

The Ringelblum Archive contains approximately 25,000 pages of testimony, artworks, literature, and correspondence.

Churns and cans
When it became clear that most Warsaw Jews would be killed, the *Oyneg Shabbes* group decided to leave their work as a witness to their lives. They buried their material in milk churns and metal boxes in three different places. The last was buried on the eve of the ghetto uprising.

Unearthing a find
The Nazis discovered the *Oyneg Shabbes* leaders and shot them. The only leader to survive the Holocaust was Hersz Wasser, Ringelblum's assistant. He remembered where some of the churns and cans were buried and in 1946 helped dig them out (pictured right). A second cache was unearthed in 1950, but the third was never discovered.

Sifting and sorting
The library where the *Oyneg Shabbes* group used to meet is now the site of the Jewish Historical Institute. Here, archivists from the Institute are sorting through some of the material found in the rusty churns soon after it was discovered. The material had been buried quickly and was in poor condition when it was dug up.

Scream the truth
Dawid Graber was 19 when he helped to bury the first cache in August 1942. It contained this page, his last will and testament. It was damaged by damp, but under a microscope, the writing is clear: "I would love to see the moment when the great treasure will be dug up and scream the truth at the world… May the treasure fall into good hands, may it last into better times, may it alarm and alert the world."

77

THE MURDER OF THE VICTIMS

THE DELIBERATE KILLING of people who the Nazis believed had no right to live became known as the Holocaust. Various methods were used to make these murders ever more systematic and efficient. Between 1933 and 1945, more than 10 million men, women, and children were murdered – about six million of these were Jews and about half a million were Romanies.

Cattle cars
The majority of people deported to labour and death camps were transported in cattle wagons, such as this one. Inside, conditions were desperately cramped and the air was stifling. Many died on the way.

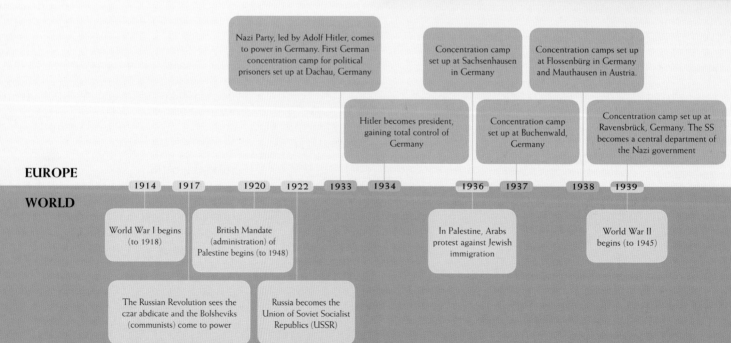

Nazi Party, led by Adolf Hitler, comes to power in Germany. First German concentration camp for political prisoners set up at Dachau, Germany

Concentration camp set up at Sachsenhausen in Germany

Concentration camps set up at Flossenbürg in Germany and Mauthausen in Austria.

Hitler becomes president, gaining total control of Germany

Concentration camp set up at Buchenwald, Germany

Concentration camp set up at Ravensbrück, Germany. The SS becomes a central department of the Nazi government

EUROPE

1914 1917 1920 1922 1933 1934 1936 1937 1938 1939

WORLD

World War I begins (to 1918)

British Mandate (administration) of Palestine begins (to 1948)

In Palestine, Arabs protest against Jewish immigration

World War II begins (to 1945)

The Russian Revolution sees the czar abdicate and the Bolsheviks (communists) come to power

Russia becomes the Union of Soviet Socialist Republics (USSR)

Camps set up at Chelmno, Majdanek, and Auschwitz-Birkenau in occupied Poland, and at Terezin (Theresienstadt), now in the Czech Republic. Massacre of 33,771 Jews at Babi Yar, Ukraine

Camp at Bergen-Belsen, in Germany, becomes a concentration camp

Nuremberg war crimes trials of Nazi leaders begin in Germany

Nazi plan to deport Europe's Jews to Madagascar, off the coast of Africa, abandoned. Camp set up at Auschwitz in Poland

At Wannsee Conference, Berlin, Nazis commit to the "Final Solution". Camps set up at Belzec, Treblinka, and Sobibor in Poland. *Einsatzgruppen* (Nazi killing squads) enter Soviet Union

Germany invades and occupies Hungary. Mass deportation of Hungarian Jews to Auschwitz. Romania withdraws from the war

1940   1941   1942   1943   1944   1945   1948

Japan bombs American ships in Pearl Harbor, Hawaii, USA

USA drops atomic bombs on Hiroshima and Nagasaki, Japan

USA enters World War II

Jewish State of Israel declared. Arab-Israeli War begins (to 1949)

THE ROAD TO THE DEATH CAMPS

THE WORD HOLOCAUST usually evokes images of mass murder in gas chambers. While it is true that most victims were killed in this way, it was not the original Nazi plan. The idea of death camps probably came gradually. Early in the Holocaust, victims were killed in smaller numbers, less regularly, and using several different methods, and this paved the way for the death camps.

Unworthy of life?

The Nazi code name for the enforced killing of mentally or physically handicapped people – or "life unworthy of life" – was *Aktion T4*. The Hartheim Institute, above, was one of six hospitals where the Nazis killed people by gas, gun, or lethal injection. About 275,000 people were murdered under *Aktion T4*.

Concentration camps

Many people were imprisoned in concentration camps. The majority, such as these women in Plaszów, Poland, had committed no crime. In 1933, police and storm troopers began to set up camps in Germany, and by 1939 there were six large camps and other smaller ones.

Slave labour

The Nazis treated their victims as slaves – they were a despised source of free labour. Most of the work in concentration camps was hard, dirty, and unsafe. The Nazi policy was to work people to death, so victims survived for only as long as they were fit. These men in Flossenbürg, Germany, were made to quarry heavy stones

Mobile killing units

Special units run by the SS and the police were set up to murder Jews. Called *Einsatzgruppen*, they followed the German army's invasion of other countries, including Poland and the USSR. Here, *Einsatzgruppen* have forced Jews to dig a pit and then shoot them so they fall into an open grave. It is estimated that *Einsatzgruppen* killed 1.4 million Jews.

Reinhard Heydrich

The *Einsatzgruppen* chief commander was Reinhard Heydrich. He believed that killing the Nazis' victims should not be delayed. He had various nicknames, including "The Butcher of Prague", "The Blond Beast", and "The Hangman". He was assassinated in Prague in 1942 and received a state funeral, with full honours, attended by Hitler.

Gas vans

Einsatzgruppen wanted more efficient means of killing than shooting or starving their victims. They adapted vans by sealing off the front compartment and piping exhaust fumes into the back compartment. They loaded their victims into the back and drove them to a trench or grave. The victims died within half an hour.

It is estimated that the Nazis established more than 15,000 concentration camps in the occupied countries.

ONE DAY AT JÓZEFÓW

On 13 July 1942, General Wilhelm Trapp told 500 German policemen to kill 1,800 Jews in Józefów, Poland. He added that no one would be forced to take part, but only 12 did not. The others rounded up the elderly, mothers with babies, and children, before taking them to a wood. The policemen shot them one by one. Some policemen made Jews kneel with their hands up and, smiling, posed for the camera alongside their victims. Many people think that those who did such killing must have been "obeying orders", but that was not always the case – and certainly not that day at Józefów.

CONCENTRATION CAMPS GERMANY

Camp locations in Germany 1933–45

☐ Large camp
○ City
▣ Smaller camp
— Bordering country

German camps

Most concentration camps in Germany were labour camps, but some were collection points where people were held before being moved to another camp. Others were temporary holding places for the dying. By 1939, hundreds of small camps had been merged into seven large camps, including Mauthausen in annexed Austria.

DENMARK

NETHERLANDS

BELGIUM

FRANCE

SWITZERLAND

ITALY

Ravensbrück

Bergen-Belsen

Sachsenhausen Berlin

Buchenwald

Flossenbürg

Nuremberg

Dachau

Munich

Mauthausen

PROTECTORATE OF BOHEMIA AND MORAVIA

SLOVAKIA

HUNGARY

CROATIA

0 km   100   200   300
0 miles   100   200

CONCENTRATION CAMPS were first set up in 1933. Initially, their purpose was to hold "undesirables" and political opponents of the Nazis. However, some families with children were also detained in concentration camps. Although the main purpose of the camps was not to kill people, many died because their health was neglected or they were treated brutally. In all the camps, the detainees were dehumanized and treated as mere objects.

CAMP	OPERATED	PRISONERS	DEATHS
Bergen-Belsen	1943–45	unknown	70,000
Buchenwald	1937–45	250,000	56,000
Dachau	1933–45	200,000	30,000
Flossenbürg	1938–45	>100,000	30,000
Mauthausen	1938–45	195,000	>95,000
Ravensbrück	1939–45	150,000	>90,000
Sachsenhausen	1936–45	>200,000	100,000

OCCUPIED EASTERN TERRITORY

GENERAL GOVERNMENT (OCCUPIED POLAND)

Forced labour
Prisoners worked long hours at least six days a week, often in difficult, dirty, or dangerous conditions. As well as construction sites and quarries, there were workshops and factories that made items for the German government. In 1938, the SS began using forced camp labour for profit.

A poor diet
There was never enough food for the prisoners. The food was always the same, so people did not get a balanced diet and some starved to death. These women at Mauthausen are lining up for soup, usually made with potatoes and cabbage. The other main food was bread.

Medical experiments
Some camps used detainees to test new products and procedures. For example, experiments to investigate how much pain people could endure in a compression chamber occurred at Dachau in 1942. The findings would assist the German Air Force, but the research was painful for the participants. This Romany detainee is in agony, after being forced to drink sea water to test whether it is drinkable.

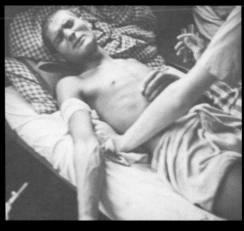

Living conditions
People were made to live in very unpleasant and unhealthy conditions. These prisoners at Buchenwald are crammed together in shared bunks, which made sleep difficult. The camps were also filthy. Most of the time there was no hot water for washing, and sometimes there was no water at all. During the summer the camps were stiflingly hot, and in the winter they were bitterly cold.

THE JEWS OF THE SOVIET UNION

JEWS HAD LIVED IN RUSSIAN LANDS for about 1,500 years, but from the end of the 19th century, anti-Semitism forced many to emigrate to the West or to Palestine. Many who stayed became involved in groups fighting for a more equal society, but even those groups were anti-Semitic. So, in 1897, Jews created their own movement, called the Bund. This revived Jewish self-confidence and developed a modern Jewish culture, still active when Russia became the Soviet Union after the revolution of 1917.

Jewish life before the Russian Revolution
For centuries, Jewish life in Russia revolved around the Jewish traditions of prayer, study, and charitable deeds. In the shtetl, the synagogue was the heart of the Jewish community, and education focused on discussing the meaning of the traditional texts, like these boys studying the Torah with their teacher.

Jews under the rule of communism
In the revolution of 1917, the Russian Empire was overthrown and the communists eventually created the Union of Soviet Socialist Republics (USSR). Many idealistic Jews believed that it would bring a better world, but anti-Semitism continued. There was no place for Jews in the new system unless they gave up their way of life. In this photo, Jews are protesting about the use of Jewish headstones for building works.

Firing squad
In June 1941, mobile killing units, called *Einsatzgruppen*, entered the Soviet Union on instructions from Nazi leader Heydrich. They were to kill Jews, communists, and other Nazi enemies. The people shot by this firing squad, and most victims, were Jews. Local people were aware of these shootings, which usually happened in broad daylight.

Areas of German and Soviet occupation

- German annexation of Austria, March 1938
- German annexation from Czechoslovakia, November 1938–March 1939
- German annexation of Memel, Danzig, and from Poland, 1939
- Hungarian annexation from Czechoslovakia, 1938–39
- Hungarian annexation from Romania, 1940
- Soviet annexation from Poland, September 1939
- Soviet annexation from Romania, 1940
- Soviet annexation of Baltic countries, 1940
- Lithuanian annexation from Poland, September 1939
- ⎯ Boundary between German and Soviet spheres of influence

Nazi-Soviet non-aggression pact

As Germany prepared to invade Poland in 1939, it signed a non-aggression pact with the USSR – an agreement not to invade or attack each other. As this map shows, they shared the areas of Eastern Europe between them. This split Poland in two. General Government was the name for the area of Poland not incorporated into the Third Reich.

```
0 km   200    400    600    800   1,000
0 miles     200         400        600
```

ESTONIA, LATVIA, LITHUANIA, EAST PRUSSIA, SOVIET UNION, GERMANY, GENERAL GOVERNMENT, SUDETENLAND, BOHEMIA AND MORAVIA, SLOVAKIA, AUSTRIA, HUNGARY, YUGOSLAVIA, ROMANIA, Baltic Sea, Black Sea

At Babi Yar, more than 33,000 Jews were killed in just two days.

Babi Yar uncovered

In September 1941, Jews in Kiev, Ukraine, were herded to the Babi Yar ravine. Ukrainian police forced them to undress and walk to its edge. When German troops shot them, they fell into the abyss. The Germans pushed the wall of the ravine over, burying the dead and the living. Despite attempts to destroy the evidence, Soviet investigators discovered the bodies in 1943.

Massacre at Babi Yar

The Babi Yar massacre was the most intensive Holocaust killing. Nazis reported killing 33,771 Jews in two days, and later killed more Jews, Romanies, Soviet prisoners of war, and Ukranian nationalists. The Soviet estimate is 100,000. Police grabbed children like these and flung them into the ravine.

"They took my mother and shot her too ... and then my grandmother, my father's mother, she was eighty years old and she had two children in her arms, and then there was my father's sister. She also had children in her arms and she was shot on the spot with the babies in her arms..."

Rivka Yosselevscka, who survived the Einsatzgruppen in Zagrodski in 1942, giving evidence at a war crimes tribunal court

A mother attempts to shield the child in her arms, as she is about to be shot by the Einsatzgruppen.

THE JEWS OF ROMANIA

JEWISH ORIGINS IN ROMANIA date back to the 2nd century CE. In later centuries, Jews migrated into Romania from other parts of Europe, especially those Jews expelled from Spain. Before the Holocaust, Romania had the third largest Jewish community in Eastern Europe, and life was fairly untroubled. However, severe anti-Semitic activity after World War I prompted many Jews to leave Romania and prepare for a new life in Palestine.

Romania and surrounding regions, 1941
The territory of Romania changed during the Holocaust as regions were occupied by Hungary (northern Transylvania) and Bulgaria (southern Dobrudja). Romania occupied the Transnistria area of Ukraine in the Soviet Union, and transported Jews and Romanies there.

In Odessa and the surrounding area, 40,000 Jews were killed between 23–25 October 1942.

Iron Guard

The Legionnaires began in Romania in 1927 as an ultra-nationalistic, anti-Semitic movement, which lasted into the 1940s. Officially called the Legion of the Archangel Michael, its patron saint is shown here. In 1930, the Iron Guard was formed as a paramilitary branch of the Legion. The Iron Guard massacred Jews when Romania lost land to the Soviet Union.

Antonescu's government

In 1940, Romania became a satellite of Nazi Germany. Inspired by the Nuremberg laws, the government of General Ion Antonescu, shown here with Hitler, made 80 anti-Jewish laws and statements. It also massacred 7,000 Romanies, deporting and starving thousands of others, and killed up to 380,000 Jews – the greatest number outside Germany.

From Iasi to Calarasi

The Iasi massacre in June 1941 was the most dreadful in Romania. With rumours of the Soviets landing, an estimated 14,000 Jews were shot. The 4,330 survivors were taken in sealed cargo trains to camps at Calarasi and other places. About 2,500 died from suffocation, thirst, or starvation. When trains were stopped to remove the dead, more Jews were killed by local people.

Terror in Bucharest

For three days in January 1941, the Iron Guard and Bucharest hooligans terrorized Jews in the streets and in their homes. They arrested thousands, seizing and vandalizing Jewish property and belongings. Many synagogues were desecrated and two, including this one, were set alight. Many Jews were killed, and their bodies hung up on hooks.

The Odessa massacre

Odessa in Transnistria was part of the Ukraine. When the Germans occupied the area in late 1941, Romanians and Germans began exterminating the Jewish population of 300,000. Some were hanged in the street, some shot, and some burned alive.

Bessarabia and Bukovina

Half of the 320,000 Jews in Bessarabia and Bukovina were murdered in 1941. More than 123,000 were deported in forced marches, and on rafts like this, to death camps in Transnistria. The Germans shot some and sent the rest back. Many drowned, others died on the way, or in camps set up in Bukovina and Bessarabia.

A chance to leave

In December 1942, Romania allowed the Transnistria Jews to go as illegal immigrants to Palestine. By 1944, when Romania changed sides in the war, 13 boats had left. Two of them, including the *Struma*, shown here with 769 passengers on board, tragically sank during the voyage.

THE FINAL SOLUTION

THE NAZIS CALLED THEIR PLAN to exterminate Europe's Jews the "Final Solution". They saw the Jews as a problem that had to be solved, and the removal or, preferably, destruction of all Jews was the solution they wanted. Although they had already murdered more than a million Jews, the Nazis still thought of other ways to kill them more quickly and efficiently.

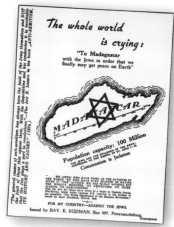

The Madagascar Plan
In 1940, the Nazis had the idea of taking over France and moving large groups of Jews to the French colony of Madagascar, off Africa. But the plan required the British navy to transport the Jews and, because Britain had not been defeated, the idea was scrapped.

AKTION REINHARD

The plan to exterminate Polish Jews was code-named *Aktion Reinhard* – named after Reinhard Heydrich, one of the leading planners of the "Final Solution". In order to carry out the plan, in 1942 extermination, or death, camps were built in Poland at Belzec, Sobibor, and Treblinka. This graph shows the numbers of victims murdered in each of the six main camps in Poland. Two million Jews were exterminated through *Aktion Reinhard*.

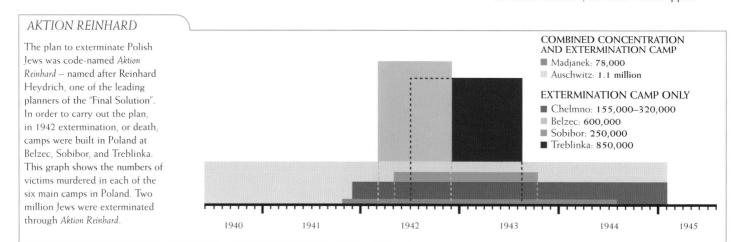

COMBINED CONCENTRATION AND EXTERMINATION CAMP
■ Madjanek: 78,000
□ Auschwitz: 1.1 million

EXTERMINATION CAMP ONLY
■ Chelmno: 155,000–320,000
■ Belzec: 600,000
■ Sobibor: 250,000
■ Treblinka: 850,000

1940   1941   1942   1943   1944   1945

At the Wannsee Conference, Estonia was marked as being Jew-free. Every one of the country's 1,000 Jews had been murdered.

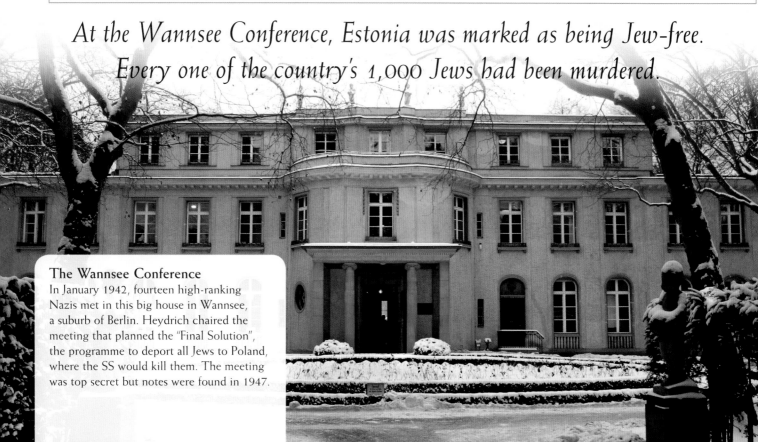

The Wannsee Conference
In January 1942, fourteen high-ranking Nazis met in this big house in Wannsee, a suburb of Berlin. Heydrich chaired the meeting that planned the "Final Solution", the programme to deport all Jews to Poland, where the SS would kill them. The meeting was top secret but notes were found in 1947.

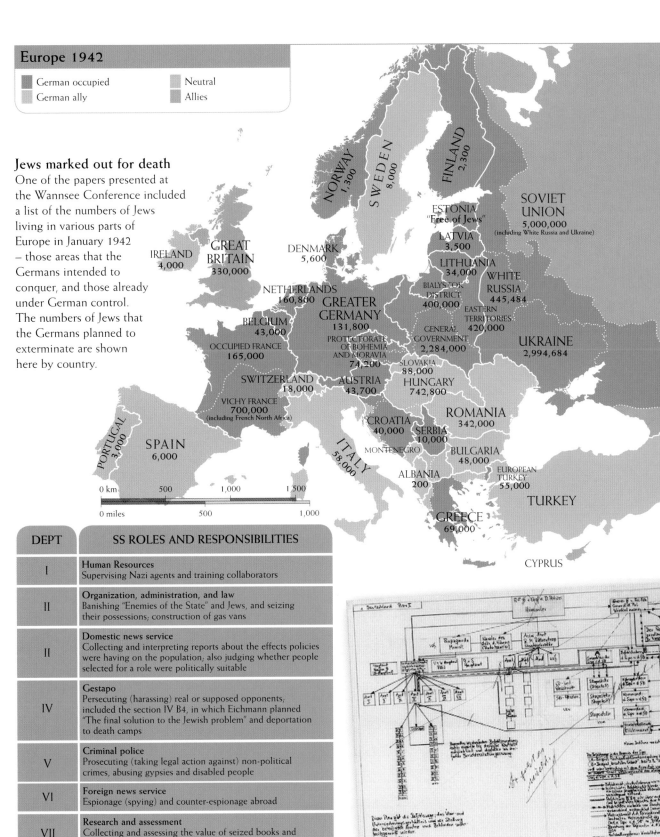

Europe 1942

- German occupied
- German ally
- Neutral
- Allies

Jews marked out for death

One of the papers presented at the Wannsee Conference included a list of the numbers of Jews living in various parts of Europe in January 1942 – those areas that the Germans intended to conquer, and those already under German control. The numbers of Jews that the Germans planned to exterminate are shown here by country.

NORWAY 1,300
SWEDEN 8,000
FINLAND 2,300
ESTONIA "Free of Jews"
SOVIET UNION 5,000,000 (including White Russia and Ukraine)
LATVIA 3,500
IRELAND 4,000
GREAT BRITAIN 330,000
DENMARK 5,600
LITHUANIA 34,000
WHITE RUSSIA 445,484
NETHERLANDS 160,800
BIALYSTOK DISTRICT 400,000
GREATER GERMANY 131,800
BELGIUM 43,000
EASTERN TERRITORIES 420,000
OCCUPIED FRANCE 165,000
PROTECTORATE OF BOHEMIA AND MORAVIA 74,200
GENERAL GOVERNMENT 2,284,000
UKRAINE 2,994,684
SWITZERLAND 18,000
AUSTRIA 43,700
SLOVAKIA 88,000
HUNGARY 742,800
VICHY FRANCE 700,000 (including French North Africa)
CROATIA 40,000
SERBIA 10,000
ROMANIA 342,000
MONTENEGRO
SPAIN 6,000
PORTUGAL 3,000
ITALY 58,000
BULGARIA 48,000
ALBANIA 200
EUROPEAN TURKEY 55,000
GREECE 69,000
TURKEY
CYPRUS

0 km 500 1,000 1,500
0 miles 500 1,000

DEPT	SS ROLES AND RESPONSIBILITIES
I	**Human Resources** Supervising Nazi agents and training collaborators
II	**Organization, administration, and law** Banishing "Enemies of the State" and Jews, and seizing their possessions; construction of gas vans
II	**Domestic news service** Collecting and interpreting reports about the effects policies were having on the population; also judging whether people selected for a role were politically suitable
IV	**Gestapo** Persecuting (harassing) real or supposed opponents; included the section IV B4, in which Eichmann planned "The final solution to the Jewish problem" and deportation to death camps
V	**Criminal police** Prosecuting (taking legal action against) non-political crimes, abusing gypsies and disabled people
VI	**Foreign news service** Espionage (spying) and counter-espionage abroad
VII	**Research and assessment** Collecting and assessing the value of seized books and other materials

Central SS administration

The SS, short for *Schutzstaffel*, which means "protective squadron", began as Hitler's bodyguard. Under Heinrich Himmler, it grew into a force of 600,000 men, separate from the army. In 1939, the SS became a central department and Heydrich its chief. The main divisions are shown on this chart from 1940.

Nazi chain of command

The Nazi organization was extremely tightly structured, with clear lines of command between members. Adolf Eichmann ran Gestapo Department IV B4 and, at his trial in 1961, he drew this chart of the organization, which was submitted in evidence.

The pile of shoes of the victims in block 4, Auschwitz I, photographed in 1995 as an exhibit for the museum

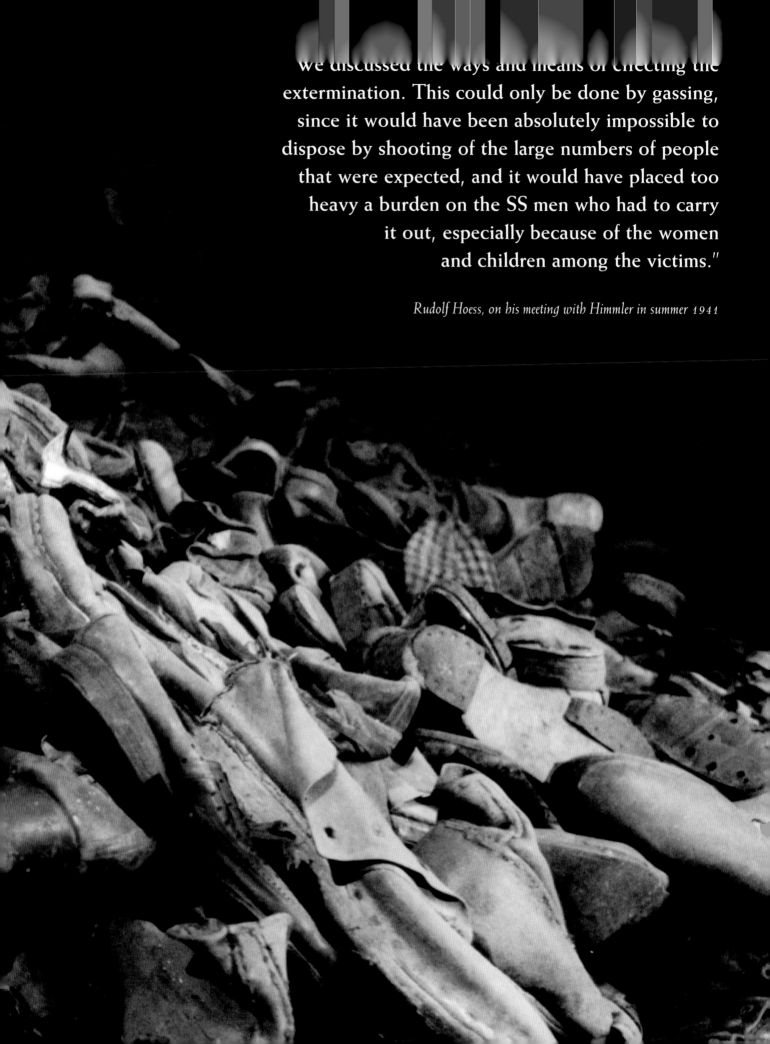

we discussed the ways and means of checking the extermination. This could only be done by gassing, since it would have been absolutely impossible to dispose by shooting of the large numbers of people that were expected, and it would have placed too heavy a burden on the SS men who had to carry it out, especially because of the women and children among the victims."

Rudolf Hoess, on his meeting with Himmler in summer 1941

LABOUR CAMPS

CAMPS WERE ORIGINALLY INTENDED to imprison the people that the Nazis most despised. But when World War II began, the purpose of the camps changed to forced labour and outright murder. By 1942, extermination through work was official policy, and prisoners in all the concentration camps were – quite literally – worked to death.

Work brings freedom
A German sign, such as the one below, hung over the gates of five labour camps. The Nazis may have used "Work Brings Freedom" seriously or as a cruel joke, but people in labour camps were definitely not free. If the Nazis thought a person was unfit and could not work they would be killed, and no matter how hard a person worked, they would never be freed.

ARBEIT MACHT FREI

A complex of camps
Many of the larger labour camps also had smaller sub-camps. This map shows the many sub-camps of Auschwitz in occupied Poland. Auschwitz and Majdanek were labour and extermination camps where inmates died from illness, injury, exhaustion, or gassing.

WARTHEGAU

GREATER GERMANY

LOWER SILESIA

UPPER SILESIA

GENERAL GOVERNMENT

Hubertushütte
Eintrachthütte   Bismarckhütte
Laurahütte
Blechhammer   Lagischa
Neustadt   Hindenburg   Kattowitz
Gleiwitz   Sosnowitz & Fürstengrube
(I,II,III&IV)   Althammer   Neu Dachs
Günthergrube   Chelmek   Kunzendorf
Charlottegrube   Kobior   Janinagrube
Lichtewerden   Babitz   Bobrek
Altdorf   Auschwitz II
Freudenthal   Tschechowitz   Auschwitz III
Plawy   Auschwitz I
Golleschau   Raisko
Jawischowitz
Harmense
Budy

SUDETENLAND

PROTECTORATE OF BOHEMIA AND MORAVIA

SLOVAKIA

0 km	25	50	75	100

0 miles	25	50

The growth of camps
Nazi labour camps held prisoners from almost every country in Europe. From 1939, there was a huge rise in the number of camps and prisoners. The SS claimed there were more than 700,000 prisoners in camps by 1945. This aerial view shows the scale and organization of the camp at Majdanek in Poland.

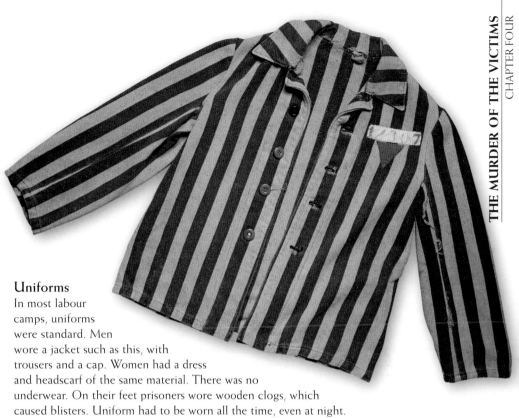

Stolen property

Prisoners at labour camps had all their belongings taken away. Money and valuables, sentimental items such as photographs, and practical items such as spectacles were confiscated. Valuables were sold to make money for Germany, such as these wedding rings taken from women at Buchenwald in Germany.

Uniforms

In most labour camps, uniforms were standard. Men wore a jacket such as this, with trousers and a cap. Women had a dress and headscarf of the same material. There was no underwear. On their feet prisoners wore wooden clogs, which caused blisters. Uniform had to be worn all the time, even at night.

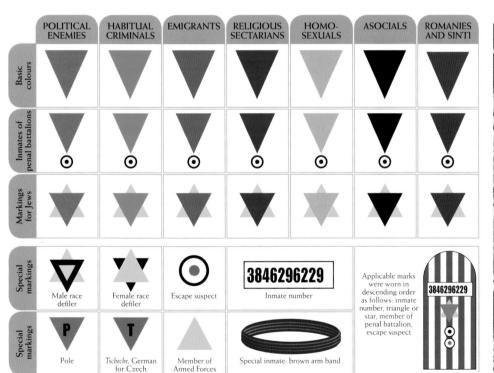

Numbers and badges

Each prisoner had a number, which was sewn onto their uniform. Guards and other officials called prisoners by their numbers, instead of their names. Other cloth badges, shown here, were used to identify where a prisoner came from and why the Nazis selected them for the camp. An inmate would usually have at least two symbols, but could have more than six.

Types of work

Prisoners carried out different tasks in labour camps. Most of the work involved hard labour, such as clearing this site in Dachau. Some people worked in factories, producing items to support the German economy or ammunition to support Germany in the war.

COLLABORATION

THE TERM COLLABORATION usually refers to cooperation or partnership. However, from 1940 in France, collaboration took on a sinister new meaning when it was used to describe people who cooperated with enemy occupiers. This negative use of the word spread. During the Holocaust, collaboration with the Nazis took many forms, such as rounding up Jews for death camps or even taking part in killings. For example, Lithuanian military units, encouraged by the SS, slaughtered 5,000 Jews in public in 1941. In every country occupied by Germany, there was some form of collaboration.

Stolen and stored
The Nazis stole their victims' money, jewellery, and other valuables – even gold tooth fillings. Germany also seized the government assets of the countries it occupied. The stolen goods were converted into gold bars and held in Swiss banks.

The Vichy Regime of France
The government of Vichy in southern France cooperated with the Nazis by passing laws that defined Jews as a separate race and restricted their rights. This poster from a 1941 exhibition called "The Jew and France" used Nazi stereotypes of Jews crushing the world. Vichy authorities also helped to deport Jews and Romanies to death camps. Of the 75,000 French Jews deported, only 2,500 survived.

Persecution in Belgium
From 1940 to 1944, Belgium was occupied by the Nazis and Belgian authorities took responsibility for the deportation and persecution of Jews. They drew up a national register of Jews and gave it to the Nazis. Fascist groups carried out anti-Semitic campaigns, calling for the deportation of all Jews. Here, René Lambrichts, leader of an anti-Semitic group, is addressing a workers' union.

Collaboration in Norway
When Germany invaded Norway in 1940, Norwegian fascist politician Vidkun Quisling made himself head of the government. Germany confirmed him as Prime Minister in 1942. Quisling, pictured here at a girls' camp in 1941, ordered the Norwegian armed forces not to resist Germany. This had the effect of creating a movement in Norway to resist Nazism. Throughout the war he collaborated with the Nazis and the word "quisling" came to mean a traitor.

Grand Mufti of Jerusalem
A mufti is a Muslim scholar who specializes in Islamic law. The Grand Mufti of Jerusalem, Muhammad Amin al-Husseini, was a religious leader and Arab nationalist. He discussed the extermination of the Jews with Nazi leaders, as seen here with Hitler in 1941, in Berlin. He also helped recruit Bosnian and Albanian Muslims to fighting units in support of the Nazis. His part in the Holocaust came out in testimonies given in the trials afterwards.

The Nazis in the Netherlands
During World War II, Anton Mussert was head of the Dutch National Socialist government. Once Germany occupied the Netherlands, his government helped the Nazis by stripping Jews of their rights. Here, Mussert is receiving the *"Heil Hitler!"* salute at a celebration of the Dutch Nationalist Socialist party. In 2005, Prime Minister Jan Peter Balkenende apologized for his country's collaboration during the war.

ROUNDING UP THE VICTIMS

THE NAZIS' COLLECTION of their victims for labour or extermination required excellent organization and a complex system of transport. Victims were rounded up, often by force, and told to report to a certain place bringing only a small amount of food and some clothing. They did not know where they were going or what would happen

Nazi camps

- ☐ Labour camps
- ☐ Transit camps
- ☐ Extermination camps

NORWAY

SWEDEN

FINLAND

Grini
Bredtveit (1942)
Berg (1942)

Klooga
Valvara
Lagedi

IRELAND

UNITED KINGDOM

DENMARK

Horserød

Kaiserwald

OCCUPIED EASTERN TERRITORY

SOVIET UNION

Skarzysko-Kamienna

Stutthof

NETHERLANDS
Westerbork
Bergen-Belsen
Vught

Neuengamme
Ravensbrück
Sachsenhausen
Dora-Mittelbau

Poniatowa
Koldichevo

Chelmno

Treblinka
Majdanek
Sobibor
Trawniki
Belzec

Mechelen
Breendonk
Compiègne
Drancy
Pithiviers

BELGIUM

Buchenwald
Fünfbrunnen
Flossenbürg

GREATER GERMANY

Gross-Rosen

PROTECTORATE OF BOHEMIA AND MORAVIA

GENERAL GOVERNMENT

Janowska

Natzweiler-Struthof

Auschwitz

Budzyn
Starachowice

Vittel
Schirmeck-Vorbruck
Dachau
Mauthausen

Plaszow

FRANCE

SWITZERLAND

Bolzano

SLOVAKIA

HUNGARY

Gurs

Fossoli di Carpi

San Sabba

ROMANIA

Rivesaltes

Sajmiste

CROATIA
Schabatz
SERBIA

PORTUGAL

SPAIN

ITALY

MONTENEGRO

Nisch

BULGARIA

ALBANIA

TURKEY

Salonika

GREECE

Camps in Europe

The Nazis rounded up victims by first taking them to a transit camp. These camps were temporary and people were not usually forced into hard labour. At this stage, they had no idea that conditions where they were heading would be much harsher. The map above shows some of the Nazi camps in occupied Europe. Although there are three types of camps, some had more than one function.

False sense of security

Westerbork transit camp was set up after Germany occupied the Netherlands in 1942. Jews deported to Westerbork were destined for one of five concentration or extermination camps. They were lulled into a false sense of security because of the shops and other features of normal life there. Jews were even allowed some of their religious customs, such as lighting candles for Hanukah, shown here.

Drancy transit camp
Although there were no ghettos in Western Europe, the camp at Drancy, near Paris, was like a ghetto. The buildings were like prisons, and there was severe overcrowding. Food was in short supply and served communally. Most Jews were taken from Drancy to Auschwitz and murdered on arrival.

The ghetto-camp of Terezin
In 1941, the Nazis turned the prison in Terezin into a cross between a ghetto and a camp and renamed it Theresienstadt. When the Red Cross asked to inspect a camp, Terezin became a showcase, as shown by these Jews sitting in a fake café. For these visits, the Nazis also arranged concerts, football or tennis games, and other activities to make it seem a happy, healthy place.

About 15,000 children passed through the Terezin ghetto between 1941 and 1944. Only about 100 of them survived the Holocaust.

The Red Cross comes to check
The conditions were better in Terezin than in concentration camps, but not as good as the Nazis pretended. This 12-year-old girl's painting shows how deceitful the Nazis were. The Red Cross inspectors' vehicles are arriving in Terezin – and the Nazis are quickly ordering everything to be brightened up.

VOICES
TRANSIT CAMPS

Having travelled for several days in the terrifying and cramped conditions of the cattle trains, for many Jews the transit camps confirmed their fears of what was to come. Some stayed in the transit camps for months, others were there for just a few days before being moved on yet again.

"I REMEMBER GETTING to the camp and I was screaming all the time. I was scared and I was all alone in the middle of a mass of children and people. In the camp we slept on the floor sitting up anywhere, and we were given soup and bread. We were all thrown together, adults with children, but then the children got separated. I was there for only four days and I feel I was there for four years. They were the longest days."

"EVERYWHERE THERE WERE guards and dogs – big dogs. I don't know who barked louder – the dogs or the Germans – but they sounded the same. They couldn't speak. They would never speak to us. They would bark. They did everything to degrade us. They decided when we had to go to sleep. It could be two in the afternoon or midnight. They came in and they said, 'This is what we want you to do. Do it.' That's all. And to go to the restroom we had to wait in line. There weren't enough restrooms. There was no means to have a shower, for sure. It was smelly. It smelled very bad."

"I THINK THERE must have been a couple of hundred children there. Most of them were so frightened that they couldn't even talk. There was a strong smell of urine because the children got scared and they urinated on themselves. Or they couldn't wait to go to the restroom or whatever, but we were very scared, everybody was very, very frightened."

Michelle Cohen-Rodriguez
(Born in France, 1935)
Michelle remembers the fear
of the hundreds of children in
Drancy transit camp.

"EVENTUALLY, I THINK it was after three days and three nights, we arrived in a place called Atachi... a border town on the River Dniester... The unloading of the train was a very traumatic experience because everything had to be done fast and they were shouting and we were slipping and we were full of our own excrement and we ended up in this large field in the rain. From the train to the field I think there was some walking. But I remember the field where there were a lot of people who had been deported before us and they had already been in this field a number of days and you slept in the mud and there was no food and, as bad as we looked, those people looked a lot worse because not only had they been brought there in trains the same as we were but on top of that they had slept in the mud for several days, and there was no food and they were cold and the clothes and the shoes, everything was mud and they looked like bewildered people. A lot of them were people from Bessarabia, and my mum and I visited my aunt in Bessarabia before and the people were elegant and they wore hats and I couldn't understand what they were doing in this field. I mean, why did they leave their homes? Why did they leave their gorgeous clothes and their gorgeous hats? What are they doing here? What's happening? Everything became unknown from the way life used to be before, when we knew exactly what every minute in every day will bring. Suddenly every minute was a total unknown thing. And not only did we not know what was going to be but we knew that it was going to be bad. Whatever we didn't know, we knew it was going to be bad."

"AT ONE TIME or another there were some very famous people in Westerbork. In the Concertgebouw orchestra, all the violinists were Jewish. So at one time they picked them all up and brought them to Westerbork and then the Germans asked them to give a concert. They probably thought that if they gave concerts for the Germans they would be deferred. Unfortunately, if I remember rightly, I think only one violinist survived. Then there was a famous Jewish boxer who was well known. He used to do boxing exhibitions for the Germans. That was a crazy situation when you think about it. It was a camp where next week you might be dead but the Germans came and watched an exhibition of boxing or they had a concert or they had plays performed to entertain them... The whole camp was the size of a big football field, maybe a little bit bigger, but there were 20 or 30 thousand people at a time there. That's how confined it was."

Felicia Carmelly
(Born in Romania, 1931)
Felicia was just ten years old when she and her mother were sent to Atachi camp.

Fred Spiegel
(Born in Germany, 1932)
Fred was sent to Westerbork camp in the Netherlands in 1943 and remained there for several months.

DEATH CAMPS

THE NAZIS BUILT SIX CAMPS for the purpose of carrying out mass murder. All the camps were based in Poland at Auschwitz, Belzec, Chelmno, Majdanek, Sobibor, and Treblinka. Auschwitz and Majdanek also functioned as labour camps. Most people killed in the death camps were Jewish, but there were large numbers from other groups, especially Polish people in Majdanek and Romanies in Belzec and Auschwitz-Birkenau.

On arrival

People arriving at the death camps were faced with harsh conditions and brutal treatment, yet many had no real idea of what would happen. These Romany families at Belzec death camp are waiting for instructions from their captors. They will be stripped of everything – their clothes, their belongings, their names, and their lives.

Transport to the camps

Most people arrived at the camps by train. Those who survived the journey were often weak and sick. Artist and Holocaust survivor David Olère painted *Arrival of a Convoy* in which prisoners drag a heavy cart of corpses to be buried or burned. More prisoners are arriving on the train behind.

Security and control

Death camps were surrounded by walls or electrified fences, with high watchtowers, like this one at Sobibor. The inmates were under the constant watch of the guards, who would often beat, torture, or kill them for no reason.

Disguise and deception

Most camps were built in isolated areas. The Nazis kept their true purpose hidden to prevent panic or anger among the victims. Those sent to gas chambers were told they were showers. Deception was especially strong at Treblinka, as this plan shows, with its station sign, fake ticket office, zoo, and garden.

Killings by shooting

Guards often shot prisoners for minor offences, such as disobeying an order or stealing food. If someone escaped, some of the inmates still in the camp were killed as a punishment and to discourage others from attempting to escape. This woman, in light clothing, has been taken into the snow at Belzec to be shot.

Killing in gas vans

These people in Chelmno death camp are about to enter one of the gas vans that were permanently stationed there from 1941. Chelmno was the first of the camps to use poison gas as a means of taking life. Among the many victims killed there were the 250,000 Jews from the Łódź ghetto.

More than 66,500 Warsaw Jews were killed at Treblinka in its first month.

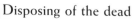

Gas chambers

Gas vans were replaced by larger, brick gas chambers, which also used carbon monoxide. Later, Zyklon B was developed to kill inmates, and it came packaged in tins such as these. Pellets were dropped through the ceiling of the gas chamber. Zyklon B was safe for the guards to handle, but death was slow and agonizing.

Disposing of the dead

Some of the inmates were forced to remove dead bodies from the gas chambers. At first, corpses were buried, but Nazi leaders felt that cremation – burning the bodies – was more efficient and more hygienic. Crematoria were built, resembling hot "ovens" large enough to take more than one body. Here billowing smoke is seen rising from the crematoria in Majdanek.

LIFE IN THE CAMPS

THE SQUALID CONDITIONS and the brutality of the guards made life in camp a degrading and dehumanizing experience. Extermination camps were filled with the sights, sounds, and smells of people dying, and the remaining inmates lived in constant fear of being killed. The captors saw their victims as increasingly inhuman, which made it easier to kill them. More and more people died in these horrific circumstances.

A sense of death
Inmates who were fit and healthy when they arrived at camp were chosen for labour and would live a little longer. The young, sick, or old faced immediate death. In this painting, French Holocaust survivor David Olère shows victims who are doomed to die.

Camp routines
The armed guards who ran the camps were extremely strict, issuing orders to inmates from dawn until night. The day began with guards shouting commands and marching the people off to work, as this photograph shows. Inmates had a little time without work on Sundays but were never allowed to choose what they did.

Roll call
Camp roll call took place at least twice a day. Whether blazing hot or bitterly cold, prisoners were forced to line up outside, sometimes all day or all night, to be counted. This painting by Zinovii Tolkatchev, an artist with the Soviet forces, shows inmates on the ground either beaten or dead from exhaustion.

Sleeping conditions
Although people were permanently tired from the gruelling work, sleep was extremely difficult. Prisoners slept in bunks, such as these at Auschwitz, which were arranged in three or four tiers. The wooden slats hurt the prisoners' thin, bony bodies. Sometimes those in the top bunks did not have the strength to climb into bed.

Meal times

One of the most degrading experiences in the camp was meal time. The soup was thin at the top of the pot but thicker lower down so inmates jostled to get served from the bottom. If any soup was spilled, they scrabbled on the floor to lick it up. In these pictures by Pavel Fantl, an inmate of Terezin, in Czechoslovakia, a man is depicted wasting away with hunger. At the same time, his whole world appears to shrink around him.

One bowl

Inmates never had enough water – and the little they did have was often dirty. Sometimes people were so thirsty that they drank from puddles. Each inmate was given one bowl and this would be used for soup, for washing themselves, and often for going to the toilet at night. People guarded their bowls closely – an inmate of Auschwitz even scratched his name on his.

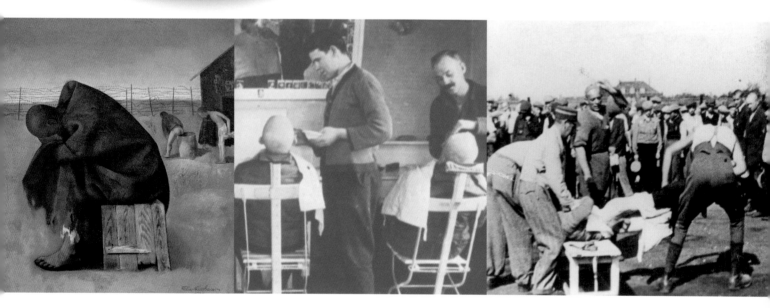

No privacy

Toilets or buckets were arranged in long rows so inmates had no privacy. Toilet bowls had no seats and rarely worked properly so the water overran with faeces and the stench was terrible. In this painting, German Jewish artist Felix Nussbaum conveys the lack of dignity of the experience.

Dirt and disease

The camps were filthy and plagued by rats. The most serious and infectious disease was typhus, carried by lice and fleas. Lice-infested detainees were often killed to avoid the spread of disease, so they would try to pick lice off their bodies. At most camps, including here at Oranienburg, in Germany, inmates' heads were shaved.

Cruel "sport"

Guards called their attacks on prisoners "sport" and they needed little provocation. They shot children in front of their mothers, brutally kicked and stamped on inmates, and hanged them by their wrists behind their back. Here, a prisoner has been forced to bend over a block to be whipped while other prisoners are made to watch.

VOICES
LIFE IN THE DEATH CAMPS

The horror of the death camps is hard to understand for most people today. For those who survived, the extreme cold, the disease, the abuse, the starvation, the loss of loved ones, and the constant fear of being sent to the gas chamber remain all too clear in their minds.

"I DIDN'T KNOW what was happening but I knew it was something terrible happening and the neighbour next to me said, 'They took her children, they took her children!' And I said, 'Where did they take them?' and she said, 'Probably to burn, they will burn them.' And I got scared, thinking, 'this woman has lost her mind. So we are going to lose our minds here?' I didn't believe that one could burn a child alive."

"THEY SENT US in to have a shower and then they shaved our heads. They gave us the striped uniforms to put on. I had a man's suit and my father quickly rolled up my sleeves and my trousers because that's all you had — the striped uniform. That striped uniform I kept until I was liberated. I was with my father — all the men were on one side and the women on the other. Then this woman walked up to me and she asked me how old I was and I said, 'I'm thirteen', and she said quickly, 'Don't say you're thirteen, say you're seventeen.' She was with the Nazis, with the SS who were walking around. So I told my father and he said, 'Then say you're seventeen if she told you!' That saved my life because the SS were walking around asking everyone, 'How old are you?' I said I was seventeen and this officer looked me up and down and he left me there, left me with my father. That was unbelievable; it was just luck that she walked over to me."

Aniela Ania Radek
(Born in Poland, 1926)
Aniela was 15 years old when she was sent to Auschwitz concentration camp.

Peter Hersch
(Born in Czechoslovakia, 1930)
Peter recalls how an SS officer in Auschwitz told him to lie about his age and as a result saved him from the gas chamber.

"*When we got* into the camp we were introduced to this overseer, who was called a *kapo* inside the camp. I asked this *kapo* when we were going to be reunited with our parents. And she pointed to one of the four brick chimneys bellowing fire and soot, and she said, 'Do you see these chimneys?' I said, 'Yes.' She says, 'There go your parents and when you go through the chimneys you'll be reunited'. I turned to my fellow prisoners and I said, 'What is she talking about? What does that mean?' Even in my darkest nightmares I could not have imagined the things that were going on there."

"*A week later* I was selected from my camp to go into another camp. It was then that I was separated from my sister, Clara. But we arranged to meet at the wires every morning at a certain place so that we could wave to each other and tell each other that we are still alive and we're still okay. Before Yom Kippur in 1944, we were worried that something was going to happen because the Nazis always had something in store during holidays or on Sabbath. I went to the wires and my sister didn't show and I thought maybe she was upset because of the holiday and I thought maybe she would be there the following morning. She didn't show then either and when she didn't come the third day I knew that something had happened to her. After the war I found out that there were big selections that day and that she was selected out to be killed."

"*Once a week* the German officers, they used to come in every barrack, they... used to go block to block and tell the women to undress... And one by one they used to pass through them, naked of course, and they were looking at you if you haven't got any disease or anything like that... And the ones that they didn't like, that had something wrong with them, they took the number and they put them in a room, completely separate from the others and then at night time they came with a truck, they took them to the gas chamber. That was every week we had to do that!... To live with that fear! Can you imagine? If someone doesn't know when they will die they are not scared, but if you know that you are going to die, that your turn will come, it's a terrible thing."

Renée Firestone
(Born in Czechoslovakia, 1924)
Renée recalls her arrival at Auschwitz, and the day she feared her sister had been killed.

Lola Putt
(Born in Greece, 1926)
Lola describes the humiliation and terror of the weekly inspections in Auschwitz.

AUSCHWITZ

IN 1940, THE NAZIS CREATED A CONCENTRATION CAMP at Oswiecim, Poland, called Auschwitz in German. The Auschwitz complex included three large camps: Auschwitz, Birkenau, and Monowitz. Auschwitz was the largest complex of camps and more than a million people were murdered there, more than at any other place.

The prison buildings
Most of the barracks were made of wood, but at Auschwitz, planned as a prison, there were brick buildings. Electrified fences surrounded the camp and separated the men's and women's blocks.

Selection for work or death
As soon as the victims arrived, they were selected for work or death. Dr Josef Mengele, nicknamed the "Angel of Death", also selected victims for his cruel experiments. These people at Birkenau have been "sorted". On the right are middle-aged men, selected for work; on the left are women, children, and the elderly, selected for death. Families were split up and never saw each other again.

Registration of the living

Each victim was given a uniform with their number sewn onto it. They were also measured, and the guards recorded their personal details. Most, like this Hungarian woman, had three photos taken. Their clothes, valuables, and other belongings were taken to warehouses, jokingly called "Kanada" – a land of plenty, far away.

Showering and disinfection

People selected to live had their heads shaved to reduce infection. The scissors were often blunt and pulled at the hair. Newcomers were also sprayed with disinfectant that made their skin sore and itchy. Then they were herded into scalding hot showers, as shown in this painting by the Polish survivor Wladyslaw Siwek.

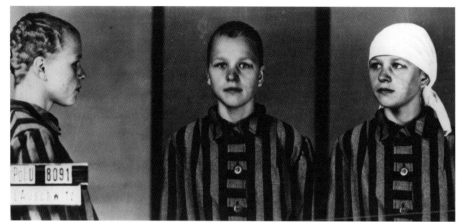

IG Farben factory

This factory was based at Monowitz, the third largest camp in the complex. IG Farben was a powerful group of German chemical companies. It was the biggest donor to Hitler's election campaign and collaborated with the Nazis throughout the Holocaust.

Tattooing

Once a detainee had been given a number, it was tattooed in black ink on the lower part of their left arm. This painful and unhygienic procedure was an attack on their person, even before they had really started life at the camp. This Italian boy, who survived Auschwitz, has been asked to show his tattooed number to the people who liberated the camp.

Mengele used about 3,000 twins, mostly Romany and Jewish children, for his painful genetic experiments. Only about 200 of them survived.

Gas chambers

The main method of killing used a chemical called Zyklon B, dropped through openings in the ceiling after the doors were sealed. Through a window, guards could watch victims dying and hear their screams. These people are walking to the gas chamber at Birkenau. They do not know what is going to happen to them.

Cremation

Prisoners called *Sonderkommando* were forced to bury the corpses, or burn them in ovens and bury the remains. Sometimes the ovens broke down or could not keep up with the volume of corpses. In the summer of 1944, when 20,000 people were gassed each day, cremation pits were dug outside.

"Driven by thirst, I eyed a fine icicle outside the window, within hand's reach. I opened the window and broke off the icicle but at once a large, heavy guard prowling outside brutally snatched it away from me. *'Warum?'* I asked him in my poor German. *'Hier ist kein warum'* (there is no why here), he replied, pushing me inside with a shove."

Primo Levi recalls the cruelty of the Nazi guards in his book, If This is a Man

The gates to Auschwitz-Birkenau, photographed in January 1995

THE JEWS OF HUNGARY

ANTI-SEMITISM IN HUNGARY had been strong since World War I, but especially so after the Nazis came to power in Germany in 1933. The Holocaust experience was different for Jews in Hungary than for Jews elsewhere. Deportations came towards the end of the Holocaust and were the most intense, with almost half a million deported in just over two months.

The "White Terror"

After World War I, the leader of Hungary, Admiral Horthy, passed anti-Jewish laws. As a result, anti-communist and anti-Semitic forces – a "White Terror" – went on a rampage, as shown in this drawing by Mihály Biró. More than 3,000 Jews were massacred, 75,000 were interned, and 100,000 fled.

Hungary and the Nazis

A number of anti-Semitic laws were passed in Hungary in 1938, even before the country was allied to Germany, Italy, and Japan in October 1940. From 1939, there was a system of forced labour. Here, Jews are being made to load, unload, and stack heavy rails. In 1941, the Hungarians handed over 17,000 Jews to German and Ukrainian forces, who massacred them.

Mass deportations

Germany invaded and occupied Hungary in spring 1944. With the co-operation of Hungarian officials and police, nearly 55,000 Jews from the provinces were deported each week. In total, 437,000 Jews, about half of Hungary's Jews, were deported. They included this woman and children, arriving at Birkenau in May 1944.

Star of David houses
Anti-Semitic laws had restricted Jews to certain areas in the capital, Budapest. Then, in June 1944, 200,000 Jews were moved into 2,000 homes, ready for the deportations that were to begin in July and August. Houses were marked with a Star of David and the Jews were forced to wear a yellow badge.

Rescue attempts
In the summer of 1944, some neutral countries and international organizations gave 25,000 Budapest Jews a protective passport and shielded them in an "international ghetto" of foreign government buildings. Here, Jews are trying to get into the Glass House, a Swiss government building which sheltered about 3,000 people.

THE ARROW CROSS

In October 1944, Germany set up the anti-Semitic Arrow Cross Party in government in Hungary. It handed over nearly 70,000 Jews for forced labour, moved all Budapest Jews into the ghetto, and tightened control of the ghetto area. Arrow Cross units, made up mainly of armed teenagers, tortured and murdered hundreds of Jews each day. This memorial of shoes on the bank of the Danube recalls the Jews who died when they were tied together, shot, and thrown into the river.

More than 550,000 Hungarian Jews were murdered during the Holocaust.

Death marches to Austria
The deportation of Budapest's Jews began in October 1944. There were not enough trains to transport the Jews to the concentration camps. Instead, many were forced to walk to Austria. This picture shows them setting out. The long journey and the cold winter, resulted in about 98,000 losing their lives by January 1945.

CLINGING TO LIFE

THE HOLOCAUST WAS ALLOWED to happen because there were very few attempts to stop Nazi plans or to save the victims. While some Jews had a chance to escape, most countries would not take them and protests from Jewish groups were rarely successful. But there were acts of great bravery as people clung to life – non-Jews who helped Jews, Jewish and non-Jewish people who fought the Nazis, and people who escaped the death camps.

Sent to safety

On the 14 July 1939, these Austrian children arrived in London as part of the *Kindertransport*. This was the transport of 10,000 Jewish children from Germany and Czechoslovakia to the UK, by a group of Jews and Christians who raised the money for their travel and accommodation.

In Germany, Nazis pass laws discriminating against Jews. Youth Aliyah founded in Germany to help Jewish children emigrate to safety

Japanese consul Chiune Sugihara issues visas to Lithuanian Jews. In Portugal, against government policy, De Sousa Mendes issues visas for Jewish refugees

Balfour Declaration in Britain – which is about to administer Palestine – favours a national home for the Jewish people in Palestine

At the Evian Conference, France, 32 nations discuss the Jewish refugee crisis. *Kindertransport* begins. *Kristallnacht* – night of violence against Jews

British code-breakers intercept a German message about the murder of Jews in the Soviet Union

EUROPE

1917   1920   1929   1933   1936   1938   1939   1940   1941

WORLD

British Mandate (administration) of Palestine begins

In Palestine, Arabs protest against Jewish immigration

Japan bombs American ships in Pearl Harbor, Hawaii, USA

In Palestine, The Jewish Agency, formed to support Jewish immigration, is recognized

World War II begins (to 1945). The ship *SS St Louis* cannot find safe haven anywhere for more than 900 Jewish refugees. In the USA, rabbis establish a rescue committee to save European Jews

In Amsterdam, Holland, Anne Frank goes into hiding. In Poland, the Zegota underground rescue organization is set up. Riegner telegram warns Allies of plans to murder Jews at Auschwitz

Two prisoners escape from Auschwitz and reveal what is happening there. Nazis offer Allies a million Jews in exchange for trucks and supplies

7,500 Danish Jews escape to Sweden. Escape attempt at Sobibor camp, Poland

25,000 Jewish prisoners taken from Germany to Sweden. Nuremberg war crimes trials of Nazi leaders begin in Germany

1942   1943   1944   1945   1948

USA enters World War II

USA drops atomic bombs on Hiroshima and Nagasaki, Japan

In Washington DC, 400 American rabbis protest at the situation of Jews in Europe. In New York, 70,000 people join a "Stop Hitler Now" rally

Jewish State of Israel declared. Arab-Israeli War begins (to 1949)

TRYING TO GET AWAY

THE NAZIS WANTED GERMANY and the rest of Europe to be free of Jews and, to encourage them to leave, made life difficult. Initially, Jews were allowed to take some money and belongings with them, but later the Nazis taxed them for leaving Germany and restricted what they could take. Some families were split up if they could not afford the emigration tax. For many German Jews it was not until *Kristallnacht* in 1938 that they realized the Nazi threat to their lives and the urgent need to escape.

Nazi policy on Jewish emigration
In 1937, the Nazis asked the British to accept a massive number of Jews into British-owned Palestine, but they refused. The Nazis later decided that more drastic measures were needed to solve the "Jewish problem". While under Nazi occupation, similar policies of forced emigration existed in Austria and Czechoslovakia. These Jews are queuing for exit visas in Vienna, Austria.

The Evian Conference
In 1938, representatives from 32 countries met in Evian, France, to discuss the issue of Jews seeking asylum. Although all of them, including Britain and the USA, expressed sympathy, they gave excuses for not taking in Jewish refugees. This cartoon in an American newspaper shows a Jew with nowhere to go.

Safe haven
Despite international reports of Nazi violence and racist laws against Jews, it was still very difficult for Jews to find a safe haven. There were very few choices for them, and even those countries that did take Jews took them in small numbers, as this chart shows.

RECEPTION OF JEWS			
Countries	Numbers	Countries	Numbers
USA	102,222	Canada	6,000
Argentina	63,500	Italy	5,000
UK	52,000	Czechoslovakia	5,000
Palestine	33,399	Sweden	3,200
France	30,000	Cuba	3,000
Holland	30,000	Spain	3,000
South Africa	26,100	Hungary	3,000
Poland	25,000	Uruguay	2,200
Shanghai	20,000	Denmark	2,000
Belgium	12,000	Norway	2,000
Portugal	10,000	Philippines	700
Australia	8,600	Venezuela	600
Brazil	8,000	Dominican Republic	472
Switzerland	7,000	Japan (unknown, several hundred)	
Yugoslavia	7,000	Mexico (unknown, several thousand)	
Bolivia	7,000		

TERRE PROMISE

The Promised Land
One name for the land of Israel and its capital Jerusalem is Zion. For 2,000 years, Jews cherished the dream of Zionism – returning to their homeland. In the 1930s, the Jewish feeling for Zionism became even stronger. This poster is for the 1935 French film *Promised Land* – about the hope of creating the land of Zion in Palestine.

British Mandate of Palestine
After World War I, Britain controlled the Palestine region of the Ottoman Empire and planned to make it a national home for Jews. These passengers on the *Patria* are fleeing the Nazis and heading for Palestine. However, many Arabs were against Jewish immigration, and in 1939 Britain restricted the number to 75,000 over five years.

Limits on liberty
Between 1933 and 1939, about 270,000 German Jews applied for immigration visas to the USA. These refugee Jewish children wave to the Statue of Liberty. However, immigration quotas, limited partly due to anti-Semitism from the public and some members of the government, meant that far fewer visas were issued.

Of more than 900 passengers on the St Louis, fewer than 300 survived the Holocaust.

Doomed voyage
In May 1939, the SS *St Louis* left Germany for Cuba, carrying more than 900 Jewish refugees, including these women. However, immigration policy had changed and the refugees were not allowed to enter. The ship sailed on to other ports but nowhere would take them. There was no choice but to return to Europe.

JEWISH EFFORTS TO RESCUE JEWS

OUTSIDE EUROPE, Jewish individuals and groups made attempts to help the Jews of Europe. They protested against Nazism, pleaded with governments to intervene, and provided welfare for Jews in the ghettos. Some helped Jews to escape, while others struck deals to try to end deportations.

The work of "The Joint"

Between 1939 and 1945, the American Jewish Joint Distribution Committee – known as "The Joint" – raised more than $70 million for Holocaust victims, providing welfare, such as orphanages, schools, and communal kitchens. The Joint also helped Jews to escape, like this boy about to board a ship in Portugal.

American rabbis

The American rabbis' 'Vaad ha-Hatzala Rescue Committee was set up in November 1939. By 1941, it had helped 650 rabbis and Jewish students reach the USA, Palestine, and Shanghai, among other places, and rescued 1,220 Jews from the Terezin ghetto-camp in Czechoslovakia. Here, in Washington DC in 1943, 400 rabbis are marching to demand President Roosevelt rescue Jews from Nazi-occupied Europe.

The Bermuda Conference

In April 1943, an international conference discussed the plight of victims of the Nazis. The Allies, fearing they might be obliged to take in Jews, agreed not to ask Germany to release refugees. Britain did not let any more Jews into Palestine and the USA did not change its immigration laws. A Jewish organization placed this advert exposing the conference in *The New York Times*.

To 5,000,000 Jews in the Nazi Death-Trap Bermuda Was a "Cruel Mockery"

When Will The United Nations Establish An Agency To Deal With The Problem of Hitler's Extermination of a Whole People?

SOMEHOW, through invisible, underground channels, one ray of shining hope might have penetrated the ghettos of Europe. A rumor might have spread and grown into a whisper among the agonised Jews of Hitler's hell. A whisper telling of deliverance from torture, death, starvation and agony in slaughter-houses. This ray of hope and this whisper were expressed in one word: Bermuda!

The rumor told of representatives of the United States and Great Britain, the leading champions of the United Nations, the protagonists of the Four Freedoms, assembling to save the hunted and tortured Jews of Europe. On the deliberations of this small convention on an Island in the Atlantic were focused all the hopes of the doomed Jews of Europe; those, too, of the free well-meaning people the world over. Men and women of good will everywhere at last believed that the United Nations had decide d to do something about the unprecedented disaster of an era of ...

The Jewish Agency

This organization encouraged Jews to settle in British Palestine. It saved 50,000 Jews through a deal whereby Germany "exported" Jews and seized their money as payment. The agency also organized illegal immigration to Palestine. In 1939, the British confined the 850 refugees from Romania on this ship, the *Parita*.

Saving young Jewish people

An important project of the Jewish Agency was Youth Aliyah (immigration). In 1934, it began to save Jewish children from difficulties and dangers, to educate them and bring them to live in Palestine. Before the Holocaust, about 5,000 were educated in boarding schools and children's villages there. The agency also rescued young people from Nazi Germany, including those here.

HANNAH SZENES

Born in Hungary in 1921, Hannah Szenes believed that the Land of Israel was the real home of the Jewish people and she went to live in Palestine at the age of 18. She joined the British Army and bravely volunteered to parachute into Hungary to collect information about Nazi activities and rescue Jews. Although the Nazis captured and tortured her, she never surrendered or betrayed her comrades. The Nazis executed her by firing squad in 1944.

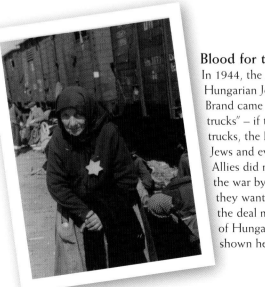

Blood for trucks

In 1944, the Nazi leader Adolf Eichmann and Hungarian Jewish activists Joel and Hansi Brand came up with the idea of "blood for trucks" – if the Allies sent the Nazis 10,000 trucks, the Nazis would spare one million Jews and evict them from Europe. But the Allies did not want to help the Nazis win the war by supplying trucks, neither did they want one million Jews. The failure of the deal meant the continued deportation of Hungary's Jews, such as this woman shown here on her arrival at Birkenau.

The Europa Plan

Deportations from Slovakia began in 1942, and these Jews were among those deported. However, when Jewish activists bribed an SS officer with $40,000–$50,000, the deportations ended. They decided to try the idea elsewhere and the Europa Plan was hatched: Jews of the world would pay $2–3 million for the Nazis to end all deportations in Europe. Tragically the plan failed because Jewish organizations could not get banks to transfer money to Nazi-occupied countries.

THE WORLD'S EFFORTS TO RESCUE VICTIMS

THE GOVERNMENTS OF MOST COUNTRIES did very little to rescue victims of Nazism by helping them to escape or giving them refuge. When they did offer sanctuary, it was often to people who had useful skills or were famous for their talent. But some governments, organizations, and individuals showed compassion by reaching out to the victims – and saving many lives.

Frank Foley
In the 1930s, Englishman Frank Foley was working at the British Embassy in Berlin. Acting alone – but with the knowledge of the British government – he issued visas for countries under British rule to Jews desperate to leave Germany. Many of the 10,000 he saved had no idea who had saved them.

Saving children
After *Kristallnacht* in 1938, a group of British Jews, Quakers, and other Christians asked the government if they could bring children to Britain for safety. The *Kindertransport* (transport of children) was allowed as long as private citizens paid all costs. Half the children went to institutions like the one below, and half to foster families.

Into the unknown
The *Kindertransport* children left by train, boat, and coach for a country that was strange to them. All the children had to wear identity labels. Some children were very young and had never been away from home. Most never saw their parents again.

Between December 1938 and September 1939, the Kindertransport *organized travel and shelter for* 10,000 *refugee children. In* 1940, *Britain interned* 1,000 Kindertransport *children as "enemy aliens".*

Safety in Sweden
Count Folke Bernadotte, representing the Swedish Red Cross, managed to persuade the Nazis to release some prisoners from German concentration camps. In March and April 1945, 36 Swedish Red Cross buses transported 25,000 prisoners to safety in Sweden. Among them were several thousand Jews, including these women who had been imprisoned in Ravensbrück.

Escape from occupied Denmark
In 1943, the Nazis planned to deport all 7,500 Jews from occupied Denmark. So Danish fishermen, determined to save the Jews, quickly ferried them to neutral Sweden in their boats. German patrols meant these night crossings were highly dangerous, but 99 per cent of Danish Jews were saved.

Jews in Albania
Almost all 600 Albanian Jews survived because so many Albanian officials agreed to forge their documents. Christian and Muslim Albanians also hid individuals and families, like this father and son. Albania offered shelter as well to Jews who escaped into Albania from Serbia, Austria, and Greece.

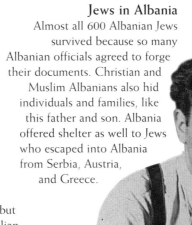

Help from Italy
Jews formed a small, but important, part of Italian society. Many survived the Holocaust because some Italian officials and private citizens obstructed deportations and helped Jews to escape. This photo shows Jewish women arriving on the island of Rab, in Italian-occupied Yugoslavia. Italian officials brought them to this isolated spot for their protection.

VOICES
THE KINDERTRANSPORT

Many hundreds of children escaped the persecution and terror of the Holocaust by being sent on trains to England. However, being separated from their parents at such a young age was in itself a traumatic experience for the children. Many of them had no idea whether they would see their parents again or not. Some were happy in their new families, but others were very homesick.

"There were parents and there were children. There were a lot of tears, there was a lot of hugging and kissing but parents were steeling themselves to put their children on the train and send them away."

"Prior to the war breaking out I received a card daily from my mother. Whether I'm well, whether I'm all right, whether I get enough to eat. Do I get enough to drink? Do I sleep well? Do I change my clothing and my underwear? Things mothers worry about. Do I get on with the people? Are they nice to me? Am I well looked after? As she finished one card she must have started another one. And every day with every card I cried myself sick. I cried myself to sleep every night, for many years. The homesickness was terrible. I remember going to a small cinema in Westbourne Grove when I was still in the hostel and they were playing a film called The Great Waltz, *which was about the life of Johann Strauss. It showed pictures of Vienna, which I knew well, and I sat in that cinema crying bitterly. People near me must have wondered whether I'd gone off my rocker."*

Emma Mogilensky
(Born in Germany, 1923)
Emma left her home in Germany in 1939 and travelled on a *Kindertransport* train from Munich to London.

Eric Richmond
(Born in Austria, 1924)
Eric recalls visiting the cinema in London after he arrived on the *Kindertransport* and missing his home and his parents terribly.

"It must have been May 1939. We were sitting at a table having dinner and my mother's plate remained untouched. She suddenly pushed her plate away and looked at Father and said, 'I heard today that both Vera and Eva can go to England,' and there was a deathly silence. My father suddenly looked very pale and drawn and he buried his face in his hands, and then he sighed and said, 'Alright, let them go'. It was a very strange moment. After that I was filled with excitement and apprehension — I didn't know anyone from our town who had ever been to England! Suddenly my sister and I assumed great importance and it seemed like a big adventure and yet, we were both going to different places. I was going to a family in Liverpool and my sister to a school in Dorset. Many years later when I discovered the man who organized the transports and saved our lives, many people held it against him that he divided siblings. He said, so wisely and so rightly, 'If I'd waited for a family who was willing to take two refugee children for unlimited time, you probably wouldn't be here today.'"

"I was taken into an empty room and left standing there, I mean can you imagine, just before my eleventh birthday, waiting there for someone you are going to be living with, who'll be in charge of your life, who you've never met. There was just a little chair there and my rucksack and I stood there and waited for the door to open and in she came! This little lady, hardly taller than myself and she had a hat on her head and it was all askew and she had a long Macintosh and it was buttoned up all along and big glasses and she peered at me from behind these big glasses. But her face broke into the biggest smile you ever saw and she started shouting and crying all at the same time as she ran towards me and hugged me and spoke to me words I didn't understand then but I learnt since that they were, 'You shall be loved.' And loved I was."

Vera Gissing
(Born in Czechoslovakia, 1928)
Vera left Prague with her sister in 1939.
Although they were sent to different
families in England, Vera was happy.

HIDING AND HELPING JEWS

MANY JEWS WERE SAVED by non-Jewish individuals and groups who saw them as human beings with a right to life – even though these non-Jews risked punishment and possible death if the Nazis caught them. As well as courage and compassion, they showed resolve by not accepting Nazi beliefs about Jews and in devising ways to help. Jews call them Righteous Among the Nations and everyone can take inspiration from their love and moral courage.

In the most unlikely places
Jews were often hidden in extraordinary places, such as barns, cellars, attics, and rooms with false walls or trap doors in the floor. This table was created to hide a Jew sheltered in Rome, whenever there was someone around who could not be trusted.

A rescue network
Under the guidance of their Christian minister, the villagers of Le Chambon-sur-Lignon, France, never betrayed a single Jew on the run. In their homes and farms, they hid about 5,000 Jews, including those shown here. Their network guided Jews to safety in Spain or Switzerland.

Between 1943 and 1945, Oskar and Emilie Schindler saved 1,200 Jews by employing them in their factories.

VISAS FOR LIFE

Aristides de Sousa Mendes
In 1940, refugees in Bordeaux, on the French coast, hoped to escape by sea. Aristides de Sousa Mendes, the Portuguese consul, was asked by Rabbi Krueger (left) to issue visas. Although the Portuguese government forbade this, Mendes issued visas for 30,000 families, a third of whom were Jewish. He lost his job and died in poverty.

Chiune and Yukiko Sugihara
Some Jews in Lithuania could buy visas for Dutch island colonies, and they asked Chiune Sugihara (the Japanese consul in Lithuania) for transit visas. Ignoring government orders, for 29 days in the summer of 1940, he and his wife Yukiko handwrote and signed more than 300 visas a day. They saved 6–12,000 lives, although it cost Sugihara his job.

Raoul Wallenberg
In 1944, when Hungarian Jews were being deported, Raoul Wallenberg was a Swedish diplomat in Budapest. His mission was to obtain Swedish passes that could help save Jewish lives. Nazi-controlled Hungary agreed to 1,500, but he bargained for 4,500, then issued three times more. Eventually he was kidnapped and never seen again.

The work of Zegota

Zegota was Poland's only underground organization of Jews and non-Jews and saved 4–6,000 Jews. Irena Sendler smuggled Jewish children out of the Warsaw ghetto in body bags so the Nazis would think they were corpses. When Jewish children changed their names, she put their real names in a jar and buried it – for later.

The secret annexe

In 1942, the Frank family went into hiding in the Netherlands with four others. Their secret annexe was very cramped and the younger daughter, Anne, shared this room with a middle-aged man. The diary Anne kept conveys the fears of living in secret, and the self-sacrifice of the non-Jews who kept them alive for two years.

Oskar and Emilie Schindler

As a member of the Nazi party, Oskar Schindler often socialized with top-ranking Nazis, and was able to bribe or persuade them that he needed Jews for his factory in Poland. His wife, Emilie, sold her jewellery to buy medicine, and looked after the sick in the clinic she set up. They saved 1,200 people, who call themselves Schindler-Jews.

NUMBER OF RIGHTEOUS	
Poland	5,941
Netherlands	4,726
France	2,646
Ukraine	2,139
Belgium	1,414
Hungary	671
Lithuania	630
Belarus	564
Slovakia	460
Germany	427
Italy	391
Greece	265
Serbia	121
Russia	120
Czech Republic	115
Croatia	105
Latvia	100
Austria	85
Moldova	71
Albania	63
Romania	52
Switzerland	38
Bosnia	34
Norway	26
Denmark	21
Bulgaria	17
Great Britain	13
Sweden	10
Macedonia	10
Armenia	10
Slovenia	6
Spain	3
Estonia	3
China	2
USA	2
Brazil	2
Chile	1
Japan	1
Luxembourg	1
Portugal	1
Turkey	1
Georgia	1
Total	21,310

Righteous among the Nations

This chart shows the numbers of Righteous among the Nations who had been identified by 2006. The Danish Underground requested that all members be counted as one, so 21 means the Danish Underground plus 20 other individuals.

"We removed the earth and carried it many kilometres away. Then we would steal the doors to a barn, to make the door. We even moved trees onto the top. If anyone saw us, we had to start again."

Eta Wrobel and her father escaped the ghetto liquidation by fleeing into the forest, where they set up a large partisan unit. She survived the war.

VOICES
LIFE IN HIDING

From a hole under a pigsty to a secret attic, thousands of Jewish families survived the war in hiding, helped by people who often put their own lives at risk by doing so. However the conditions were difficult and those in hiding had to live with the constant fear of being discovered.

"**T**HEY HID us in the barn where they dug out a hole, on top of which a pig stood. The hole was long enough that my mother and I could lie down, just enough so if one of us was on their back the other was on their side. We could not stand up, I think we could sit up and at night they would let us come out. It was totally pitch black. It was like a grave. At the beginning my mother would tell me stories. Afterwards she told me she told me about every book she ever read, every movie she'd ever seen but after a while I guess she started running out of stories, whatever the reason was (they also lowered food to us once a day). My days and nights got mixed up so when she was awake I was asleep and when I was awake she was asleep. So I retreated into this total fantasy world. I just lived in this make-believe world."

"**W**E HAVE BEEN pointedly reminded that we are in hiding, that we are Jews in chains, chained to one spot, without any rights, with a thousand duties…Sometime this terrible war will be over. Surely the time will come when we are people again, and not just Jews."

Anne Frank
(Born in Germany, 1929)
Anne wrote her diary of life in hiding in Amsterdam from 1942–44. After she was discovered, she was sent to Auschwitz. She later died in Bergen-Belsen.

Claire Boren
(Born in Poland, 1938)
Claire and her mother were in hiding from 1942–44, at first in an attic and later at a farm.

"**DECEMBER 7 NIGHT 1942** *Every day more and more Jews are being deported — now from one place, now from another. They say that the Germans have special personnel who go round town trying to find out where Jews are living, and they show the Germans these locations, and the Germans come and take our brothers away.*"

"**JANUARY 7 1943** *Last night my parents and I were sitting round the table. It was almost midnight. Suddenly we heard the doorbell — we all shuddered. We thought that the moment had come for us to be deported. My mother had already put her shoes on to go to the door, but my father said to wait until they ring once more. But the bell did not ring again. Thank heaven it all passed quickly. Only the fear remained, and all day long my parents have been very nervous. They can't stand the slightest noise, and the smallest thing bothers them…*"

"**WHERE WE WENT,** *I have absolutely no idea… We went to this house and if you visualize a Dutch closet in a house which stood about this high and had two doors and it had pots and pans and dishes and everything. We walked over to that closet and the woman put her foot on the floor twice — bang, bang! — like that. And she would open the little closet doors, the dishes and the pots came out, the bottom shelf came up, a ladder went downstairs and we were down the ladder. And when we came down there, there were about 14 or 15 kids down there!…we were there for about two or three weeks. It was not a very healthy environment to be in for kids but we did. If they wanted you to be quiet, if somebody was coming to the house, she would bang on the floor three times. That meant, 'not a sound!' We were trained just like seals — not a whisper, not a sneeze, not even an eyelash would move, everybody was totally quiet. If they banged on the floor twice everything is clear, then we can talk again.*"

Alexander Van Kollem
(Born in the Netherlands, 1928)
Alexander was in hiding from 1942–43, at first in a basement and later in two different farmhouses.

Moshe Flinker
(Born in the Netherlands, 1926)
Moshe wrote his diary in hiding before he and his family were arrested and taken to Auschwitz-Birkenau and gassed in 1944.

THE CHURCHES

CHRISTIANS HAVE OFTEN DEBATED whether they should be involved in political action to change the world or concentrate on changing themselves and their relationship with God. During the Nazi period, especially when the Third Reich started persecuting minorities, this debate escalated. Most European churches and individual Christians took a neutral stance. But some worked with the Nazis, while others opposed them, often at cost to their own lives. Many Christians who rescued Jews were members of religious minorities.

Hitler and the Catholic Church
The Roman Catholic Church hoped that the Third Reich would defeat communism. Hitler promised not to interfere with the Church, and Pope Pius XII agreed that the Church would not comment on Nazi activities and policies. The Church ignored Nazi atrocities and, when Jews in Rome were deported, it broke its pledge to protect them. This nun is asking for Hitler's autograph.

Jews and the churches
Any Jews who were protected by a church had to pose as Christians to avoid being discovered by the Nazis or betrayed to them. Sometimes, church congregations expected the Jews they hid to convert to Christianity. These two Jews, perhaps wearing their yellow stars for the last time, seek refuge in a church. The angle that the photographer has chosen emphasizes the perceived size and strength of the church.

"Hidden children"

Some Jewish parents saved their children from deportation by entrusting them to a Christian family or organization. "Hidden children" were instructed in Christian beliefs and always had to hide their Jewish identity. This Jewish girl, pictured with her cousin and a Catholic priest, has received her First Communion as a member of the Church.

Rescued by Quakers

The Quakers (or "Society of Friends") are a religious group that refuses to fight in any war. During the Holocaust, Quakers hid and rescued children, like these Spanish Jewish boys who are helping American Quakers in a French refugee camp. They also saved some French Jews by smuggling them into Switzerland, and took 1,000 Jewish children to the USA.

German Christians

The German Evangelical Church was the main Protestant Church in Germany. A group called the German Christians became a Nazi voice within the Church, and its leader Ludwig Müller, giving the Nazi salute above, was given the title of "Reich Bishop" in 1933. German Christians banned non-Aryans from being ministers or Church teachers and sacked anyone who had Jewish ancestors.

FIRST THEY CAME...

First the Nazis came for the Communists and I did not speak out – because I was not a Communist.

Then they came for the Socialists and I did not speak out – because I was not a Socialist.

Then they came for the Trade Unionists, and I did not speak out – because I was not a Trade Unionist.

Then they came for the Jews, and I did not speak out – because I was not a Jew.

Then they came for me – and there was no one left to speak out for me.

Pastor Martin Niemöller

The Confessing Church was led by Pastor Martin Niemöller. He said he would rather burn his church to the ground than preach the Nazi trinity of "race, blood, and soil". His statement, above, about taking a stand against injustice has become well known. He was deported to a concentration camp.

Dietrich Bonhoeffer

A leader of the Confessing Church, Dietrich Bonhoeffer believed that Jews should convert to Christianity but courageously opposed the Nazis' plans to murder Jews. This bold bronze sculpture outside his church in Berlin depicts the way the Nazis hanged him in prison, naked and kneeling. He had been captured while helping Jews escape to Switzerland.

THE ALLIES

THE ALLIES COULD NEVER HAVE IMAGINED or anticipated the full atrocities of the Holocaust – and the Nazis were careful to conceal as much information as they could. Although the Allies were partly aware of what was happening, they did not make this known to the public because of the rules surrounding "official secrets". Today, questions are being asked about why the Allies did so little to stop the Nazi massacres and possibly save millions of lives.

Families listen to radio news
In the early 1940s, there was no internet or television with up-to-the-minute news. However, in Europe, America, and other countries, many families – such as this one in the USA – had a radio at home. It was the main source of entertainment and information, and radio broadcasts also gave news of how the war was progressing.

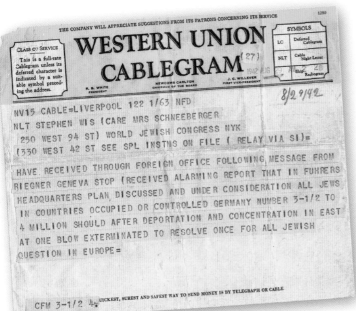

The Riegner telegram
On 10 August 1942, Gerhart Riegner, a European lawyer, sent a telegram to the British and US governments about Nazi plans to start gassing Jews at Auschwitz that autumn. A British government official sent the telegram shown here to Rabbi Stephen Wise, an American Jewish leader. For security, he sent it via the US government, but they only passed it to Wise on 29 August. On 24 November the US government announced what was happening. By then the gassings had already started.

Station X
Bletchley Park, known as Station X, was the British government's code-breaking centre during World War II. Experts worked round the clock to crack the code of the German Enigma machine, shown here. This helped intercept German messages, including one about the massacre of thousands of Jews in the Soviet Union in June 1941.

Rabbi Stephen Wise

As president of the American Jewish Congress, Rabbi Stephen Wise tried to persuade the US government to stop the massacre of Jews. But they either ignored him or said he had no evidence. In March 1943, 70,000 people came to the "Stop Hitler Now" rally organized by the American Jewish Congress in New York. Wise continued to address other gatherings (left) but, like the other Allies, the USA did not act to save the victims of the Holocaust.

The Auschwitz Protocols

In 1944, two Jews escaped from Auschwitz. They estimated the numbers already killed and warned of plans to murder thousands more. They drew this map (left) which, with sketches and descriptions, was called the Auschwitz Protocols. It was sent to Britain, the USA, and the Vatican. In September 1944, the Allies took the aerial photo of Auschwitz-Birkenau (above), showing that it could be bombed by air. It never was.

News on film

In most parts of the world, Nazi persecution and extermination of victims was a minor news event. In the 1940s, cinemas showed main films and also short news films. These newsreels, like the British Pathé Gazette, were mainly about the war and not the Holocaust. Towards the end, there was some footage of deportations, ghettos, and camps.

133

Resistance and rescue
"Let us not be led like sheep to the slaughter!" wrote Abba Kovner, an important partisan leader, in January 1942. He urged Jews to fight for their dignity rather than live in fear. This idea is expressed in Arthur Szyk's painting *Modern Moses*, in which he portrays the leader of the ancient Jews as inspiring and directing the partisans.

ESCAPE TO THE FORESTS

MANY JEWS TOOK TO THE FORESTS in Eastern Europe to avoid deportation, and some also joined the partisans – groups of people who were resisting the spread of Nazism. But some partisans would not let Jews join, so they formed their own groups. The forests were safer for the Jews because German soldiers avoided these areas for fear of attack, and tended to keep to the towns and roads.

Partisan spirit
The Yiddish song, *Zog nicht keynmol*, meaning "Never say that you are walking your last road", was composed by Hirsh Glik in the Vilna ghetto, Lithuania. His words express the partisan spirit of defiance and it became a favourite marching song. Gradually it spread beyond Eastern Europe and became known as the *Song of the Partisans*.

Sabotage by the partisans
Between 30,000 and 40,000 Jewish partisans operated in various countries. If caught, the Nazis tortured them before killing them. Most Jewish partisans were unarmed and without military experience, but were of great value to the Allies. These partisans are laying explosives on a railway where a Nazi train is due to run.

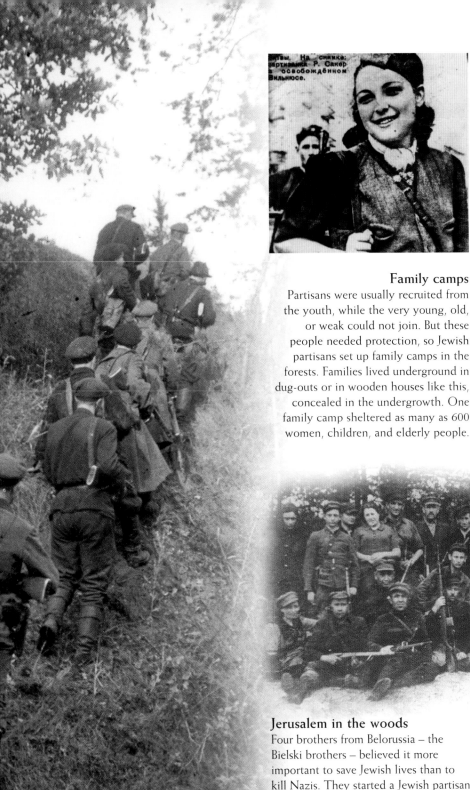

The role of women and teenage girls

Women played a vital role in partisan activities. They took responsibility for cooking as well as caring for the sick and wounded. They also acted as spies, scouts, smugglers, and couriers. A number of women, like Rachel Rudnitzki-Yuker in Lithuania, were armed and actively fought the Nazis. On several missions, women used their feminine charms to distract Nazis while male partisans were engaged in sabotage.

Family camps

Partisans were usually recruited from the youth, while the very young, old, or weak could not join. But these people needed protection, so Jewish partisans set up family camps in the forests. Families lived underground in dug-outs or in wooden houses like this, concealed in the undergrowth. One family camp sheltered as many as 600 women, children, and elderly people.

Jerusalem in the woods

Four brothers from Belorussia – the Bielski brothers – believed it more important to save Jewish lives than to kill Nazis. They started a Jewish partisan group (above), which sheltered families in their camp, known as "Jerusalem in the woods". The camp held 1,200 Jews, the largest rescue of Jews by Jews.

Life as a partisan

Staying alive was a challenge for partisans, especially in winter. Typhus, an infectious and often fatal disease carried by lice, was another risk. This boy is part of a group on the move, probably to escape danger.

CHEATING DEATH

THE NAZIS' ULTIMATE GOAL was to kill, and the victims' ultimate goal was to stay alive. In this struggle, the victims needed to cling to hope and to devise ways of cheating death. Many found an inner strength that surprised even them. Every day brought great risks, and punishment – especially in death camps – frequently meant being killed. Yet many survivors tell of camp inmates who showed the utmost bravery – even knowing the dangers.

Stealing and sabotage

Prisoners stole food whenever possible. In *The Food of the Dead for the Living,* survivor David Olère depicts himself collecting abandoned food to throw into the women's camp. Another survivor spoke of receiving some jam. Rather than eat it, he put the jam in the tank of a Nazi vehicle, hoping it would damage the engine.

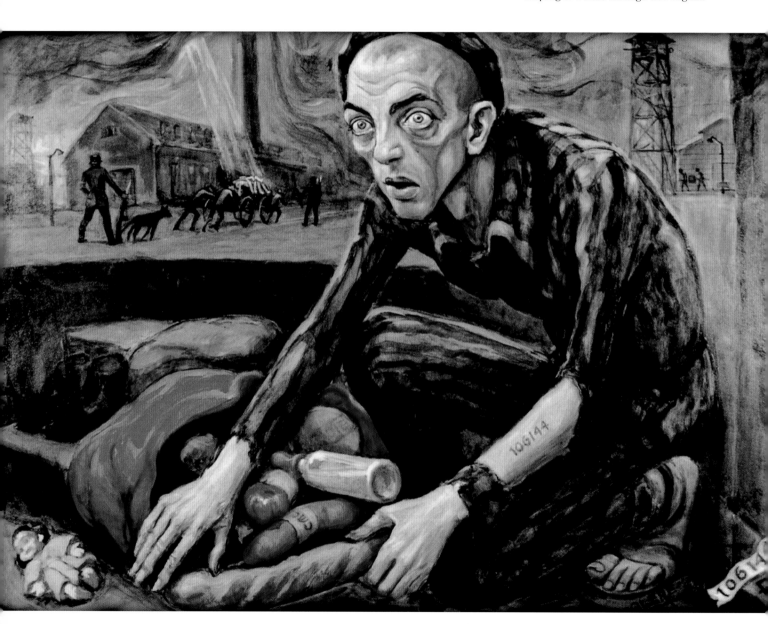

Affirming life

With death all around, inmates showed their love of life in many ways. Despite the lack of materials, some people painted flowers on the crematoria walls. This mural is from the children's barracks at Birkenau. When there was no water, one man symbolically "washed" himself with bare hands, saying that dignified people needed self-respect.

Choosing how to die

At the mercy of guards, most inmates realized that they were likely to be killed. Yet some, knowing they could not cheat death, would at least deny their captors the satisfaction of murder. This man threw himself on the electrified fence at Dachau, and took from the Nazis the power over his life.

Approximately 50 prisoners who escaped from Sobibor on 14 October 1943 survived the war.

Escape from Sobibor

In 1943, 800 inmates of Sobibor made an ambitious escape attempt. They had secretly made weapons, which they used to stab or axe several guards, so that they could grab their guns to shoot their way out. Most of the inmates were killed escaping or were captured later, but 70 survived who would otherwise have been gassed – some are shown here in 1944. The escape attempt was also a major psychological victory, and the camp closed soon afterwards.

"BE STONG AND BRAVE"

At Auschwitz-Birkenau in 1944, a group of women working in munitions began to collect tiny amounts of gunpowder while men saved boot polish tins. With these, they made "grenades" to blow up this crematorium and kill the guards. The saboteurs were also killed in the blast, but did achieve what the Allies did not even attempt. The women's leader, Rosa Robota, and three others were tortured but never betrayed their comrades. As they were hanged in view of the women, Rosa shouted "Be strong and brave!"

THE END OF THE WAR

DURING THE LAST MONTHS of the Holocaust, the conditions in the camps got worse, and the Nazis treated their victims more brutally. The Holocaust officially ended in 1945 when the Allies liberated the concentration camps, but while the war was over, problems with health and hygiene persisted. There were also questions as to where the survivors would go, whether they could be reunited with loved ones, and how they would rebuild their lives.

Liberation of Auschwitz
These children were in the camp at Auschwitz, in Poland, when it was liberated by Soviet forces on 27 January 1945. Dressed in adult uniforms, they were led from their barracks by soldiers and relief workers.

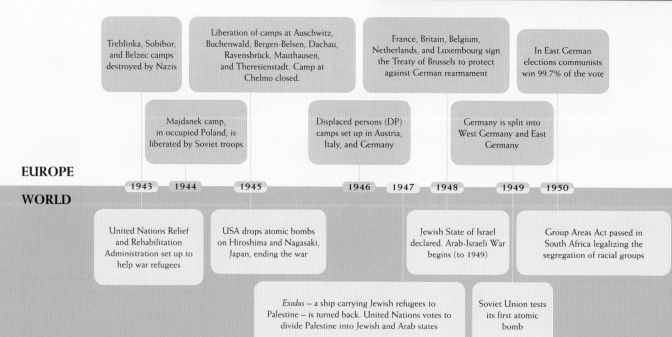

EUROPE

Treblinka, Sobibor, and Belzec camps destroyed by Nazis

Liberation of camps at Auschwitz, Buchenwald, Bergen-Belsen, Dachau, Ravensbrück, Mauthausen, and Theresienstadt. Camp at Chelmo closed.

France, Britain, Belgium, Netherlands, and Luxembourg sign the Treaty of Brussels to protect against German rearmament

In East German elections communists win 99.7% of the vote

Majdanek camp, in occupied Poland, is liberated by Soviet troops

Displaced persons (DP) camps set up in Austria, Italy, and Germany

Germany is split into West Germany and East Germany

1943 1944 1945 1946 1947 1948 1949 1950

WORLD

United Nations Relief and Rehabilitation Administration set up to help war refugees

USA drops atomic bombs on Hiroshima and Nagasaki, Japan, ending the war

Jewish State of Israel declared. Arab-Israeli War begins (to 1949)

Group Areas Act passed in South Africa legalizing the segregation of racial groups

Exodus – a ship carrying Jewish refugees to Palestine – is turned back. United Nations votes to divide Palestine into Jewish and Arab states

Soviet Union tests its first atomic bomb

Soviet troops leave Austria. Warsaw Pact is formed by communist states of Eastern Europe and Soviet Union

European Convention on Human Rights agreed; food rationing in Britain ends

Diary of Anne Frank published

The last DP camp at Föhrenwald, Germany, is closed

| 1952 | 1953 | 1954 | 1955 | 1956 | 1957 |

USA detonates the first hydrogen bomb at Enewetak, in the Pacific

Racial segregation in American schools outlawed

Alabama bus segregation laws declared illegal by US Supreme Court

Yad Vashem, the Holocaust Memorial and Education Centre, set up in Jerusalem, Israel. Soviet Union detonates hydrogen bomb

Boycott of buses in Alabama, USA, in protest at the arrest of Rosa Parks, who refused to give up her seat to a white man

In the USA, Martin Luther King leads nationwide resistance to racial segregation and discrimination

DEATH MARCHES

WHEN THE NAZIS REALIZED that enemy forces were approaching a camp, they quickly moved the prisoners on to another. They wanted to conceal the evidence of what they had done. Inmates travelled mainly on foot and, because so many died or were killed on the way, these journeys became known as death marches.

Deserted camp
The first camp to be liberated by the Allies was Majdanek, Poland, which Soviet troops reached in July 1944. The Nazis started to evacuate 15,000 prisoners in March, and the last 1,000 left the day before liberation. Many thousands of inmates' shoes were found there.

The ones left behind
Prisoners whom the Nazis thought were unfit for slave labour in Germany were not taken on the marches. These Soviet men on crutches and sticks were left behind in Majdanek because they were unable to join the death march. Altogether, about 1,500 inmates were left at camp.

Longest march
The biggest single death march was from Auschwitz. It began on 18 January 1945, nine days before Soviet troops liberated the camp. About 66,000 inmates were made to walk 56 km (35 miles) then herded into trains. One in four died from hunger and exhaustion or were killed outright. Survivor Jan Hartman was one of those on the death march from Auschwitz to Bielsko. His painting (above) depicts the brutality of the march.

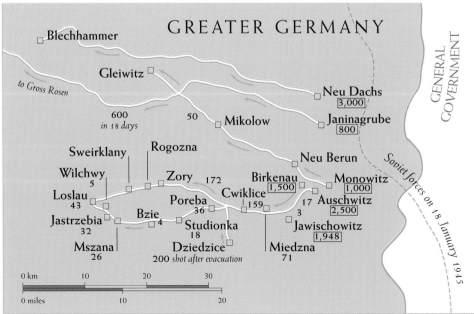

The number of deaths
This map shows the high number of deaths in just one day of marches from Auschwitz, Monowitz, and Birkenau, and sub-camps at Neu Dachs, Janinagrube, and Jawischowitz. In boxes, below the names of the camps are the number of prisoners who set out. The numbers along the way show how many died, and where.

GREATER GERMANY

GENERAL GOVERNMENT

Soviet forces on 18 January 1945

Blechhammer

Gleiwitz

to Gross Rosen

600 in 18 days

50

Mikolow

Neu Dachs
3,000

Janinagrube
800

Sweirklany

Rogozna

Wilchwy
5

Zory

172

Neu Berun

Monowitz
1,000

Loslau
43

Poreba

Cwiklice

Birkenau
1,500

Auschwitz
2,500

17

Bzie

36

159

3

Jastrzebia
32

4

Studionka
18

Jawischowitz
1,948

Mszana
26

Dziedzice
200 *shot after evacuation*

Miedzna
71

0 km   10   20   30

0 miles   10   20

Walking to live
The winter of 1944 was bitterly cold and those on the death marches were weak and hungry. The only way to survive was to keep walking, despite frostbite and blistered feet. Many people saved others by supporting them as they walked.

Death trains
Some journeys started on foot, continued by train, and ended back on foot. Prisoners were packed into open wagons usually used for cattle or cargo. This reminded them of their deportation to the camps and added to their trauma. When this train reached Dachau from Buchenwald, it contained almost 3,000 corpses.

An estimated 100,000 Jews died on the death marches.

Deeper into Germany
About 250,000 prisoners were marched from one camp in Germany to another through towns and countryside. This photograph of a death march (left) was taken from the window of a German home. Survivors say that nobody offered them food or any kind of help along the way.

Left to die
Very few people escaped from the death marches. Anyone who lagged behind was shot or beaten, while others died of exhaustion. Bodies were left behind (right). After the camps were liberated, the Allies made locals bury the bodies in the interests of public health.

VOICES
ENDURING THE DEATH MARCHES

Many thousands of people died during the death marches –
enforced walks from the camps that covered huge distances,
invariably without food or water. No one could stop to rest.
If they did, the Nazis would shoot them on the spot.

"By now I was accustomed to cruelty. I've seen and heard things happening in Auschwitz and in Birkenau. But what I saw on that march – I will never, never forget. It was pitch dark and we were marching. SS men nearby were watching us. Everyone was afraid because the moment you stepped out of the line, instantaneously you had a bullet in your head, and you just dropped wherever you were. I saw hundreds of people shot – not only Jews – there were Poles, there were people from every nationality, begging and pleading for their lives. But there was absolutely no mercy. You marched or you were dead."

"After marching throughout most of the night, I was prepared any moment just to step aside, I had had enough, I couldn't take it anymore. At that point a gust of wind blew my cap off and so in the bitter cold, my shaven head was completely uncovered. I figured I'm going to collapse any minute anyway so I may as well end my misery. As I was thinking about it, the person marching next to me kept on talking to me, encouraging me, pleading with me not to give up, 'We must survive. We can't let them get away with it.' I was crying that I was cold. Then he saw a corpse on the side with a hat, so he stepped out of the line, took off the hat and gave it to me. He risked his life for me, because he could very easily have been shot, just to make sure that I had a cap. I remember marching, sleeping and marching, and when I eventually opened up my eyes, it was daylight already. I looked around to see if I could see him but the man was gone and I was again alone and just going on like a robot."

Mayer Schondorf
(Born in Czechoslovakia, 1928)
In 1945 Mayer was sent on a death
march to Gross Rosen camp from
Auschwitz-Birkenau.

"*THEN THEY TOOK us on this march, which really was a death march. They were deliberately shooting us from the front, from the back from everywhere so there would be less people, and anybody that stayed behind a little bit, that couldn't walk so fast, they just shot him and left him in the gutter. I didn't know how far it was but since then I found out it was about 30 kilometres or 30 miles, I'm not sure which, from Gusen to Gunskirchen... You can imagine...we were dead tired from walking for miles and miles and miles, we slept always in the open... And the shooting was all night long. Shooting at us non-stop... And in the morning when they said, 'Eintreten!' ['Get up!'] I pushed my friend next to me, that I knew, that we walked together, to get up – he was dead, he was shot.*"

"*WE WENT THROUGH towns. We begged for a piece of food or water from the people – they saw us marching and they must have known the end was coming, yet nobody lifted a finger, nobody – that's something that you don't forget.*"

"*IF A person couldn't walk, or even just tripped, they shot him and left him lying there, but you kept going because you didn't dare stop to find out if the person was dead or not. We kept on walking and if you had to go to the bathroom, well unfortunately as primitive and as awful as it sounds, you just went in your pants and you kept on walking. So my mother and my sister and myself, we walked. One of us would be in the middle and the other two took the one in the middle under the armpits, so you were half dragged along by the other two and you could close your eyes and sort of doze off. The three of us rotated but I think I was the one who got most benefit of this protection because I just couldn't stay awake. We were housed overnight in a barn, which had an awful lot of hay. Finally we could lie down – it didn't matter where and how – and fall asleep.*"

Peter Hersch
(Born in Czechoslovakia, 1930)
In 1945, Peter was sent on a death march to the Gunskirchen concentration camp.

Vera Eden
(Born in Czechoslovakia, 1930)
Vera recalls how her mother and her sister helped her to keep walking on a march to Gross Rosen.

LIBERATION OF THE CAMPS

ALLIED TROOPS ENTERED Western Europe through Italy in 1943 and France in 1944, and marched towards Germany. Soviet troops took eastern Poland in 1944. The camps were still functioning when the troops reached them, but by the time Germany surrendered, the Allies had liberated almost every camp from Nazi control.

The Allies arrive
Some prisoners knew when the Allies were coming and they waved at the troops parachuting in or arriving by road. Before they could take control of a camp, the troops had to overcome the camp guards. Some inmates hugged their liberators, but the joy and relief at liberation was clouded by the death and devastation.

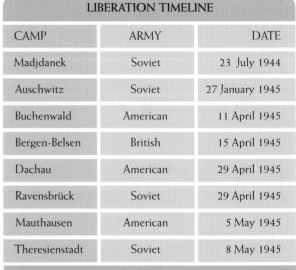

LIBERATION TIMELINE		
CAMP	ARMY	DATE
Madjdanek	Soviet	23 July 1944
Auschwitz	Soviet	27 January 1945
Buchenwald	American	11 April 1945
Bergen-Belsen	British	15 April 1945
Dachau	American	29 April 1945
Ravensbrück	Soviet	29 April 1945
Mauthausen	American	5 May 1945
Theresienstadt	Soviet	8 May 1945

Treblinka, Sobibor, and Belzec were not liberated – the Nazis destroyed these death camps in 1943. Chelmno finally closed on 17 January 1945.

Liberation dates
The chart above gives the dates when the biggest camps were liberated by the Allies, with the names of the Allied forces that freed them and the dates of liberation.

Too sick to survive

Prisoners in all the camps were weak and demoralized. Like many other survivors, this man sitting alone in Bergen-Belsen was too sick to move and was probably unaware that the camp had been liberated. After liberation, many people died from the illnesses they had suffered in camp.

The liberated prisoners were of 29 nationalities.

Record of an eyewitness

Private Zinovii Tolkatchev was with the Soviet forces liberating Auschwitz and sketched the horrors he saw there. Some of his drawings, such as this one, *A Mother and her Baby*, were done on Third Reich letterhead that he found in the Nazi offices. Perhaps his art was intended to appear as if it was an official record, by the Nazis, of the crimes they had committed.

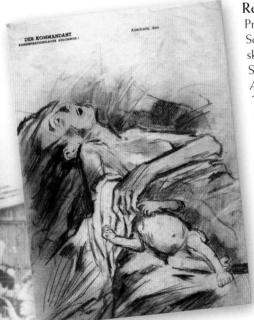

Liberators in shock

The liberating forces had no idea of the extent of Nazi crimes and the numbers of victims. Even soldiers accustomed to war had never seen such devastation and were moved to tears. Crouching beside a mass grave, this Canadian soldier is filled with shock and disbelief.

Children at Auschwitz

Of the 7,000 inmates liberated at Auschwitz, 180 were children who had been used by the Nazis for medical experiments. Some children, such as these, survived the camps, but most were orphaned and some also had no siblings left alive.

"There our troops found sights, sounds, and stenches horrible beyond belief, cruelties so enormous as to be incomprehensible to the normal mind."

Colonel William W Quinn, 7th Army,
on the liberation of Dachau

US Corporal Larry Mutinsk distributes cigarettes to inmates as they lean over the fence of the recently liberated Dachau concentration camp in April 1945.

VOICES
LIBERATING ARMIES

Many of the soldiers in the liberating armies, whether Soviet, British, or American, were deeply shocked by what they found in the death camps and the horror has stayed with them. These soldiers describe their reaction to the terrible sights they encountered during the liberation of the camps.

"*I HAVE NEVER felt able to describe my emotional reaction when I first came face to face with indisputable evidence of Nazi brutality and ruthless disregard of every shred of decency…I visited every nook and cranny of the camp because I felt it my duty to be in a position from then on to testify at first hand about these things in case there ever grew up at home the belief or assumption that the stories of Nazi brutality were just propaganda.*"

General Dwight D. Eisenhower
Supreme Commander of the Allied Forces in Europe, Eisenhower wrote this letter to his Chief of Staff, George Marshall, in April 1945, after inspecting Buchenwald in Germany.

"*WE ARRIVED IN this place called Wiemar and drove out to what I found out now, was to be a concentration camp. And I didn't know anything about concentration camps so when the officer told us to follow him and get on the trucks, I did ask him, I said, 'Where are we going?' And he said, 'We're going to a concentration camp.' And I really was puzzled because I didn't know a thing about that, no one had ever mentioned it in all the training I received, but on this day in April in 1945 I was going to have the shock of my life. Because I was going to walk through the gates of a concentration camp called Buchenwald…I could never forget that day because when I walked through that gate I saw in front of me what I call the walking dead. I saw human beings that had been beaten, starved, they'd been tortured, they'd been denied everything – anything that would make anyone's life liveable. They were standing in front of me and they were skin and bone. They had skeletal faces with deep-set eyes. Their heads had been clean shaven and they were standing there and they were holding on to one another just to keep from falling…*"

Leon Bass
American by birth, Leon witnessed the liberation of Buchenwald in April 1945 as a young private in the US army.

"THERE WAS A nasty haze over the camp and an acrid smell and there was smoke rising upwards into this haze, which was drifting upwards over the camp area. There was all barbed wire and piles of things on the side as we went through, which I believe now were shoes and suitcases and things like that. There were all these skeletons, some were walking and some were on their hands and knees. Some were just like piles of these grey-striped tunic things lying on the floor. There were some hanging onto the barbed wire, there were some all over the forecourts, which was now just plain dirt – there wasn't a blade of grass anywhere. The smell of putrefaction, urine, and faeces was absolutely everywhere. Then up towards the hospital area there were just piles and piles of naked, dead corpses outside the hospital."

"WE SAW STACKS of bodies piled up – hundreds of bodies, frozen, piled up one on top of the other. The shacks were full of bodies, and some emaciated living skeletons started to come out like shadows, walking towards us when they saw our Soviet uniforms. One man told me he was from somewhere near Warsaw. He had been in a ghetto, and been brought in to be exterminated. They worked them to death and then when they were of no more use – that was it. They shot them, they hanged them, and they gassed them. The ovens were going day and night. They just didn't have enough time to burn the bodies that were stacked up there."

"AS WE ENTERED the camp, the living skeletons still able to walk crowded around us and, though we wanted to drive farther into the place, the milling, pressing crowd would not let us. It is not an exaggeration to say that almost every inmate was insane with hunger. Just the sight of an American brought cheers, groans and shrieks. People crowded around to touch an American, to touch the jeep, to kiss our arms – perhaps just to make sure that it was true. The people who couldn't walk crawled out toward our jeep. Those who couldn't even crawl propped themselves up on an elbow, and somehow, through all their pain and suffering, revealed through their eyes the gratitude, the joy they felt at the arrival of Americans."

Jacob Sandbrand
Jacob was enlisted by the Soviet army in 1941. As a sergeant, he was involved in the liberation of several camps. During the war he concealed his Jewish identity.

Captain JD Pletcher
Captain Pletcher was in the 71st Division of the US Army at Gunskirchen in 1945.

William Williams
William was one of the liberators of Belsen in April 1945. He was there for two weeks with the British army and was responsible for organizing a food system.

CRISIS MANAGEMENT

THE WORLD HAD NEVER faced such a complex and large-scale crisis as the Holocaust. The Allies had to cope with the tragedy while still fighting the war. Military chaplains and relief agencies played important roles in the immediate tasks of rescuing survivors and controlling the spread of disease. Liberators also collected evidence to be used in the trials of Nazi war criminals.

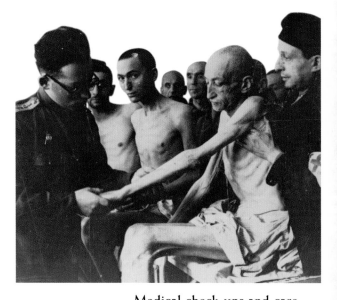

Medical check-ups and care
Disease was rampant in all the camps, and those who managed to survive were weak from lack of food. Some inmates had suffered injuries as well. Doctors and nurses visited all the camps to carry out medical assessments and determine the treatments that were needed. This Soviet physician is examining survivors at Auschwitz.

Helping the hungry
Feeding programmes were a priority. Some survivors did not have the strength to eat and nurses had to feed them by spoon. Soldiers initially gave out chocolate and tinned meat, unaware that rich food would be a shock to the system and that over-feeding could kill the malnourished.

Burying the bodies
Corpses were scattered about the camps and the liberators buried them quickly to avoid disease and distress. Using the same tools as the Nazis – shovels, wheelbarrows, and bulldozers – they buried bodies in mass graves, such as this at Bergen-Belsen.

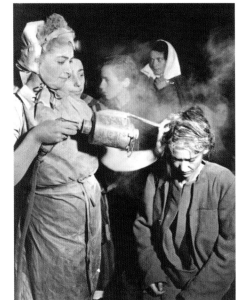

Disease and disinfection
The camps were overrun with rodents and infested with bugs. Many survivors were riddled with lice and suffered from typhus or other bacterial infections. These women at Bergen-Belsen are being sprayed with disinfectant to prevent the spread of disease. Delousing was also a priority.

Accusing and attacking
For some time, the liberators held Nazi guards as prisoners in the same camps, and their victims found this overwhelmingly difficult. Some called their torturers insulting names or hit out at them. This survivor at Buchenwald is identifying a guard who beat the prisoners brutally. They are both still wearing the same uniforms they wore before liberation.

Making the Germans see
The Allies wanted to confront German people with evidence of Nazi crimes so they could never say they did not know. This German woman is horrified at the sight and smell of people murdered by the SS near Namering, Germany. American liberators gave locals camp "tours" to see the evidence for themselves.

Making the Germans work
The Allies forced any Nazis still in camp to work. This served a practical purpose as urgent jobs were finished more quickly and the Nazis were punished in the process. Here, British soldiers at Bergen-Belsen have ordered local women to bury the Jewish dead. German civilians were also made to dig graves and bury bodies.

North Sea

DENMARK

Baltic Sea

Neustadt

Hamburg

Belsen
Hohne

Berlin

GERMANY

POLAND

Eschwege Air Base

Bad Salzschlirf

Ziegenhain
Zeilsheim

Babenhausen

CZECHOSLOVAKIA

Lampertheim

Bamberg
Bensheim

Pognitz

Burgbernheim

Fürth

Schwäbisch Hall

Stuttgart

Heidenheim

Deggendorf

Ulm
Leipheim

Biberach
Munich

St Ottilien

Landsberg

Pocking-Pine City

Feldafing

Wels
Linz

Vienna

Föhrenwald

AUSTRIA

Gabersee

Admont

Ainring

Judenburg

Bad Reichenhall

Ebensee

Saalfelden

Hallein

Badgastein

Salzburg

HUNGARY

Milan

YUGOSLAVIA

Cremona

Fossoli

Reggio

Modena
Bologna

Forli

Riccione

ITALY

Mediterranean Sea

Rome

Sardinia

Naples

Sicily

Ferramonti di Tarsia

Cosenza

| 0 km | 100 | 200 | 300 |
| 0 miles | 100 | 200 | |

Occupation zones

It is estimated that, at the peak, there were between 1.5 and 2 million displaced people in the Occupation Zones, with the highest number in the American Zone. There were DP camps in Germany, Austria, and Italy. This map shows the Occupation Zones and the locations of the major DP camps.

DISPLACED PERSON CAMPS

AS THE ALLIES TOOK OVER GERMANY and previously Nazi-occupied territories, they divided the region into Occupation Zones and managed them for several years. With the war over, Holocaust survivors found themselves a long way from home, so the Allies set up displaced person camps (DP camps) for them. Many camps were on the sites of former concentration camps, so survivors felt liberated yet not truly free.

Surviving remnant
The expression "surviving remnant" comes from the Jewish Bible. It is the belief that after a tragedy something remains and flourishes. Zinovii Tolkatchev was among the Soviet troops that liberated Auschwitz. Here, on a bleak landscape, he imagines a Jewish prayer shawl that survived destruction. Survivors called themselves and their new communities the "surviving remnant".

Zones of occupation

■ British	■ Soviet
■ French	■ American
■ Italian	■ International

Hostility at home

Many Jewish survivors returning to their home towns faced taunts and threats from non-Jewish locals. There were even outbursts of anti-Semitic violence. This photograph is taken at the funeral of 42 Holocaust survivors massacred in Kielce, Poland. Insecurity and fear made many survivors migrate west, where other survivors were based and people might be more welcoming.

UNRRA

The United Nations Relief and Rehabilitation Administration (UNRRA) was created in 1943 to help war refugees. Here, in Czechoslovakia, an UNRRA member fits shoes on Jewish orphans who are on their way to the Occupation Zones. Almost half of UNRRA funding came from the USA and was spent on resettling people in DP camps.

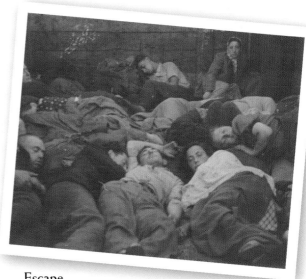

Escape

Brihah ("escape" in Hebrew) was an organization set up to help Jews escape from Eastern to Western Europe and get to Palestine by boat in secret. These young survivors are hiding in a train wagon. Funded by the "Joint" in the USA, *Brihah* was run by Holocaust survivors in Europe and by Jews in Palestine. In 1946, a network of stopping points was put in place through the American Zone.

Hope for a new land

Jewish survivors wanted a safe place to live freely. The USA was an option but immigration controls were tight. They dreamed of new lives in Palestine, but few were let in. Despite this, Jews such as this woman in Germany learned skills for nation-building.

TRYING TO BUILD A NEW LIFE

FOR HOLOCAUST SURVIVORS, the relief and joy at being alive were mixed with feelings of sadness for those who died and anger towards the Nazis for the suffering they caused. Although survivors were physically and mentally scarred by their experiences, most were determined to build a new life.

Rush of weddings

In the months after liberation, there were thousands of weddings, with about 20 each day at Belsen, the largest Displaced Person (DP) camp. A wedding was a major event for the community of a DP camp. This Jewish couple are marrying under a traditional canopy.

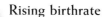

Rising birthrate

Babies were a sign of hope for the rebirth of the Jewish people. By the end of 1946, Jewish DP camps had the highest birthrate of any Jewish community in the world. Almost one-third of Jewish women aged between 18 and 45 were expecting a baby or had just given birth. As a result, baby clinics were very busy places.

Back to education

Children in concentration camps had experienced a disrupted education or had not even started school. Immediately after the Holocaust, they had to make up for lost time. These Jewish children are studying traditional religious texts in a DP camp. They also studied maths and languages.

Learning skills

For adults and young people, preparing for a new life meant gaining or relearning skills. In some DP camps, the Organization for Rehabilitation and Training (ORT) set up programmes, such as this sewing workshop in Landsberg, Germany. As well as helping people with their careers, these courses helped to build self-confidence.

Cultural life

Social and cultural activities, such as theatrical and musical events, were arranged to help Holocaust survivors rebuild their lives. For health and enjoyment, there were sports and games, as well as the ice-cream treats seen here in the Föhrenwald DP camp in Germany.

Searching for family

The Holocaust separated many families. There was uncertainty about who had survived and where people were. The United Nations and Jewish organizations collected testimonies from the victims and information about the location of survivors. These Jews in China are scanning lists of other survivors to find their loved ones.

Religious life

Rabbis among the survivors, and in Jewish relief agencies, played an important role in religious guidance. Liberation brought the freedom to pray together and celebrate festivals, such as this play to mark Purim, at Wittenau DP camp in Berlin. Religion was a way for some to assert their Jewish identity and express the pain of the Holocaust.

Finding family

Some survivors were successful in tracing their relatives and friends. International and Jewish organizations made arrangements for emotional and long-awaited reunions. Many of those who had no surviving relatives were found new families. Here, Diane Popowski, a Jewish girl from Luxembourg, hugs Renée Pallares, whose family adopted her after she was rescued from a camp.

155

SURVIVORS' DESTINATIONS

IT TOOK MANY YEARS TO RESETTLE THE SURVIVORS, who would make their new lives in countries all over the world. The biggest single number of Jews went to Palestine, which in 1948 became the State of Israel. For Holocaust survivors, and other Jews, Israel represented the fulfilment of their dream to be a free people. It became a haven for Jews everywhere.

HIAS

The Hebrew Immigrant Aid Society (HIAS) grew out of the organizations that helped Jews migrate to the USA from 1881 onwards. The Jewish immigrants above were displaced persons in Europe whom HIAS helped to settle in American society, along with many other Holocaust survivors.

Survivors sent back

The *Brihah* (escape) movement had used boats to smuggle survivors into Palestine. In 1947, however, the *Exodus* left Marseilles for Palestine but the British sent it back. The French authorities did not let people disembark and the *Exodus* was forced to sail to Germany, where survivors went to DP camps.

Detention camps

The fate of the passengers of the *Exodus*, and other restrictions imposed by the British, provoked international outrage. In response, the British stopped sending boats back and placed the passengers in detention camps instead. These women, in a detention camp on Cyprus, are pitching their tents.

UN Partition Plan

- Jewish zones
- Arab zones
- International zone

Partitioning Palestine

Under British administration, eastern Palestine was made an Arab region, called Transjordan. In the west lived Jews and Arabs. However, the Arabs were against Jewish immigration. It was a tension the British could not resolve. In 1947, the United Nations voted to divide Palestine into an Arab region and a Jewish region (both made up of three zones), and one international zone. The Arabs did not accept this motion.

LEBANON · Damascus

SYRIA

Mediterranean Sea

Haifa

Tel Aviv

Jerusalem · Amman

Gaza

EGYPT

Sinai

TRANSJORDAN

SAUDI ARABIA

| 0 km | 100 | 200 | 300 |
| 0 miles | 100 | | 200 |

The State of Israel

While Arab leaders rejected the UN Partition Plan, Jewish leaders reluctantly accepted it and prepared for a Jewish state in the three zones. On 14 May 1948, the British left and Jewish leaders declared the independence of the State of Israel. Jews danced in the streets parading flags. At dawn, neighbouring countries began dropping bombs on Israel – the Arab-Israeli war had begun.

By 1950, more than half the Jewish survivors of the Holocaust were living in Israel.

SURVIVORS	
COUNTRIES	NUMBERS
United States	c. 4,800,000
Israel	608,000
Romania	430,000
Germany	330,000
Western Soviet Union	300,000
Hungary	300,000
Poland	225,000
Canada	c. 200,000
France	200,000
Bulgaria	50,000
Czechoslovakia	44,000
Belgium	40,000
Italy	35,000
France	35 000
Baltic States	25,000
Holland	20,000
Greece	12,000
Yugoslavia	12,000
Danzig	8,000
Austria	7,000
Denmark	5,500
Finland	2,000
Britain	1,000
Luxembourg	1,000
Norway	1,000
Albania	200
Rhodes	161
Crete	7

New destinations

The chart above lists the many destinations of Holocaust survivors, and the number that had entered each area by 1945.

New life in the land

The State of Israel faced an enormous task. It was at war for the first year, absorbed hundreds of thousands of Jews arriving from many countries, and was short of money. A top priority was agriculture so that the growing nation could be fed.

The last DP camp

For some survivors, the arrangements for their new homes and new lives took many years to complete. Föhrenwald displaced persons camp in Germany, shown here, was operational until 1957 when it became the last of these camps to close.

157

VOICES
STARTING LIFE AGAIN

After liberation, the suffering continued for many people, some of whom needed medical care after starvation and disease in the camps. Many were homeless and keen to try and locate loved ones from whom they had been separated, not knowing whether they had survived. Others still wanted to leave Europe completely and many thousands settled in Israel, North America, and Australia.

"When we were liberated I didn't believe it. We had to go touch the soldiers! But it was true and we were sent to France first by truck, then they took us in an aeroplane — in a military aeroplane. In Paris the Jewish Committee took care of me, and I wanted just to retrace my route from when we went over to Italy, I thought, maybe I'll find my parents. My mother was left in France when we went to Italy, she was left in the camp. I went to Nice and in Nice there was a Jewish Committee and there was a girl there I knew from before. We embraced and she said, 'Sigi! Where have you come from?' They all thought I was dead. And she told me at once that my mother was alive in Toulouse — just a few hours away by train. Then I heard that my father was alive in Italy, that my brother was in Palestine — also saved — and my sister was in America! So the first thing the Committee did was to tell my mother that I'm alive and on the way to see her. A few days later I arrived in Toulouse. When the car drove to the house, my mother, she was on the second floor looking out from the window, we were both looking, and you know, we couldn't talk of course. Then I just ran up and we embraced."

Sigi Hart
(Born in Germany, 1925)
After liberation, Sigi obtained French papers and was delighted to be reunited with his mother in Toulouse, France.

"IT WAS HARD to decide to leave Germany and go to the United States. I was really hesitating because this is not an easy thing – I had just been through hell and of course Germany at that time was still hell right after the war. I had to have permission from my older brother – I was not even 21! My family said, 'What have you got to lose? If you're not happy there you've just got to let us know we'll send you a ticket and by hook or crook we'll get you back here. But if you're happy there then maybe you could start a different life over there for yourself.' But it was a big decision to make. It's not easy, I wouldn't recommend it. Not after what we went through as a family. It's not easy, it never went away, it is always there and it's the same with my sisters or my brothers. But the shared experience is such a tie, such a bond. We were so grateful for a new chance and, although a lot of people grow up and grow apart, we grew still closer."

"I DECIDED TO go back home to be with my cousins. I came home to Loza, in Czechoslovakia, and I said to my neighbours, 'I remember my mother said she left certain things there with you and I'd like them back.' I was looking for the silver – I didn't want anything else but they didn't have it. Then I went to my neighbours next door and they had two daughters, lovely girls – I used to go to school with them. They said, 'Stay the night, sleep the night at our place and you've still got your property, it can be built and the fields are there…', but I said to them, 'This is the last time that I'll ever step foot in this place. I'm leaving and I'll go to the other end of the world!' Not even knowing I would end up in Australia! I said, 'I never want to come back here again or see this place.'"

Julia Lentini
(Born in Germany, 1926)
Julia recalls the difficult decision of deciding to emigrate to the United States and leave behind her family.

Peter Hersch
(Born in Czechoslovakia, 1930)
After searching for family in Romania and Hungary, Peter went back to Loza, before finally emigrating to Australia.

THE AFTERMATH

THE HOLOCAUST ENDED IN 1945, but its effects continue to be felt. In the decades since, there have been attempts to compensate the victims and to bring the perpetrators to justice. It is also important that the Holocaust is never forgotten, so that such a tragedy might not be repeated. Visiting Holocaust sites, creating memorials, and learning about the Holocaust are ways to keep the memory alive so that some good may come from it.

Memorial near Mauthausen
There are many memorials to those killed at Mauthausen camp in Austria. These stone heads stare out from the roadside. The majority of inmates there were political prisoners. Jews did not arrive in large numbers until 1944 when the deportation of Hungarian Jews began.

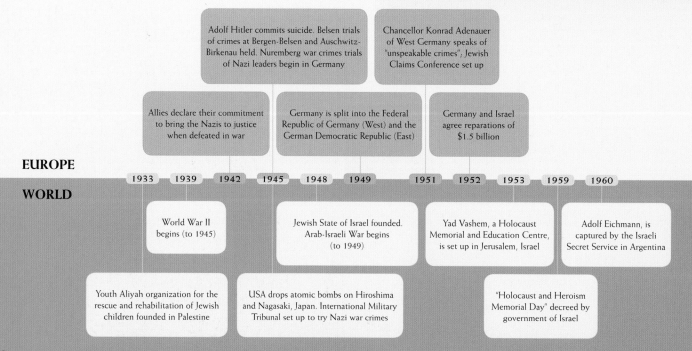

Adolf Hitler commits suicide. Belsen trials of crimes at Bergen-Belsen and Auschwitz-Birkenau held. Nuremberg war crimes trials of Nazi leaders begin in Germany

Chancellor Konrad Adenauer of West Germany speaks of "unspeakable crimes"; Jewish Claims Conference set up

Allies declare their commitment to bring the Nazis to justice when defeated in war

Germany is split into the Federal Republic of Germany (West) and the German Democratic Republic (East)

Germany and Israel agree reparations of $1.5 billion

EUROPE

1933   1939   1942   1945   1948   1949   1951   1952   1953   1959   1960

WORLD

World War II begins (to 1945)

Jewish State of Israel founded. Arab-Israeli War begins (to 1949)

Yad Vashem, a Holocaust Memorial and Education Centre, is set up in Jerusalem, Israel

Adolf Eichmann, is captured by the Israeli Secret Service in Argentina

Youth Aliyah organization for the rescue and rehabilitation of Jewish children founded in Palestine

USA drops atomic bombs on Hiroshima and Nagasaki, Japan. International Military Tribunal set up to try Nazi war crimes

"Holocaust and Heroism Memorial Day" decreed by government of Israel

The Swiss announce discovery
of 4.68 million Swiss francs
in dormant accounts from
Holocaust victims

Trial of former
Nazi, Klaus Barbie,
in France

Swiss government announces
$5 billion humanitarian
foundation from dormant
accounts of Holocaust victims

David Irving loses court case
in London in which he claims
he was wrongly accused of
"Holocaust denial"

1,564 Torah scrolls are discovered
in a Prague warehouse and
brought to London

First Christian
crosses appear at
Auschwitz

NATO bombing campaign
attempts to halt Serbia's
persecution of ethnic Albanians
in Kosovo

Germany assists with the
opening of Nazi files on victims
of the Holocaust. Pope Benedict
XVI visits Auschwitz

1961 1964 1967 1968 1974 1977 1987 1994 1997 1999 2000 2006

Six Day War
between Israel and
Arab nations

US government admits that victims'
goods, stolen by the Nazis, were
taken by US forces in 1945

In Jerusalem, Eichmann
is tried and convicted of
"Crimes against Humanity"

Assassination of Martin
Luther King, in Memphis,
Tennessee, USA

Genocide in Rwanda –
500,000 Tutsis are
massacred by Hutu

COUNTING THE COSTS

THE NUMBER OF COMMUNITIES and institutions destroyed in the Holocaust is fairly easy to count but the effect of their loss is hard to measure. The figures of 10 million people killed – including six million Jews – are often quoted. In truth, the exact figures may never be known because so much evidence was lost. Hitler, for example, burned his papers before he committed suicide. There are countless victims of the Holocaust whose stories may be lost forever.

The Czech Memorial scrolls

Fearing that deserted Czech synagogues would be plundered, Jewish leaders in Prague proposed to the occupying Nazis that religious treasures be brought to Prague's Jewish Museum. These included many Torah scrolls, which ended up in an abandoned synagogue after the war. In 1964, a deal with the Czech authorities brought 1,564 scrolls to Westminster Synagogue in London. Over the next 40 years, most scrolls were returned to synagogues across the world.

Recording evidence

The Nazis valued efficiency and precision, so they kept very detailed records of their actions, including official photographs. Individual Nazis would often take photographs of other Nazis abusing their victims and save them as personal mementos. The German film-maker Leni Riefenstahl (above) made propaganda films for the Nazis, but later some of her films would be used as evidence of Nazi plans.

Evidence destroyed

Towards the end of the war, the Nazis tried to cover up crimes that might bring them shame. They burnt Treblinka, for example, and planted potatoes on the site. Evidence was also lost when camps were looted. The Allies burned buildings to stop disease spreading, such as here at Bergen-Belsen, in Germany, where there was typhus.

Numbers of Jews killed

- none
- 0–1,000
- 1,001–10,000
- 10,001–100,000
- 100,001–1,000,000
- more than 1,000,000

Deaths during the Holocaust

This map gives the figures for Jewish deaths. Other groups selected for death are not included here simply because there are no reliable figures. These include: Soviet prisoners of war – 3.3 million estimated, Romanies – figures vary from 250,000 to 1 million, homosexuals – unknown, but 5,000 and 15,000 sent to camps, and Jehovah's Witnesses – 1,400 estimated.

NORWAY 728
SWEDEN
FINLAND 11
ESTONIA 1,000
IRELAND
GREAT BRITAIN
DENMARK 77
MEMEL 8,000
LATVIA 80,000
LITHUANIA 135,000
NETHERLANDS 106,000
GERMANY 160,000
FREE CITY DANZIG 1,000
POLAND 3,000,000
SOVIET UNION 1,000,000
BELGIUM 24,387
LUXEMBOURG 700
FRANCE 83,000
CZECHOSLOVAKIA 217,000
RUTHENIA 60,000
BUKOVINA 124,632
BESSARABIA 200,000
SWITZERLAND
AUSTRIA 65,000
HUNGARY 200,000
NORTHERN TRANSYLVANIA 105,000
PORTUGAL
SPAIN
ITALY 8,000
YUGOSLAVIA 60,000
ROMANIA 40,000
BULGARIA
MACEDONIA 7,122
THRACE 4,221
TURKEY
ALBANIA 200
GREECE 65,000
KOS 120
RHODES 1,700
CRETE 260

0 km   500   1,000   1,500
0 miles   500   1,000

THE LOSS OF LIFE

In many ways, numbers, especially very large numbers, mean nothing to us. What matters is each and every human being who was murdered by the Nazis. Each had a name, a family, a home town, and a culture. Each had a past and a present – and would have had a future. Each had their own hopes and fears, as well as memories and dreams. Just like Settela Steinbach, a Romany girl, pictured here looking out from a transport wagon on its way to Auschwitz concentration camp, Poland, in 1943.

Loss of learning

All that remains of the once majestic synagogue of Tarnów, Poland, is the central structure, now set in a park. Thousands of synagogues, Jewish schools, and community centres were destroyed in the Holocaust and, with them, much of the learning and laughter that had been at the heart of Jewish life in Eastern Europe.

Access to evidence

After the war, the German government made an archive from surviving Nazi records, but only the Red Cross had permission to see it. However, Germany came under pressure to give access to everyone and in 2006 the world's largest Holocaust archive, the International Tracing Service, opened. The racks hold 50 million records detailing Nazi victims of the Holocaust.

Going back

Survivors desperately hoped to be reunited with family members from whom they had been separated. For most people, their home town seemed an obvious meeting point. However, many who returned to pick up their old lives met with anti-Semitism from local residents. This Jewish home in Łódź, Poland, broken into and vandalized by local people during the Holocaust, is one of many homes that were ransacked or occupied during the owner's absence.

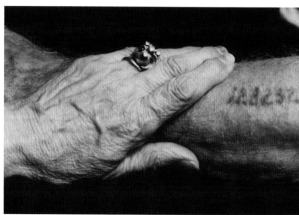

Starting again

Some survivors tried to forget their horrors, but others felt that their experiences were a part of them that had to be lived with. Some of those tattooed in Auschwitz had their numbers removed, but others, like Solomon Radasky, decided to leave them there. His numerals – 128232 – add up to 18, the number value of the Hebrew word for "life". Radasky, who might have been murdered, values this as a symbol of his rebirth as a person.

NEW BEGINNINGS

SURVIVORS NEEDED TO PICK UP THE PIECES of their broken lives, while still grieving for loved ones and suffering from their own horrific experiences. Many had lost everything, and most had to adjust to a new country. Their personal responses were varied and complex. Some resolved to live life to the full, while others were unable to enjoy anything again.

Youth Aliyah

Aliyah is the Hebrew word for "going up", and means going to live in the Land of Israel. In 1944, the Youth Aliyah programme began to help Israel's immigrant children, whether they had arrived as refugees during the Holocaust or as survivors afterwards. Its youth villages offered children companionship, education, a healthy way of life, and the care of adults. These children are learning folk dancing, one of several chances to have fun again.

Haunting memories

Many survivors were so haunted by their experiences that they found it difficult to adjust to life afterwards. They experienced sleeping problems and recurring nightmares, in some cases for the rest of their lives. Tamara Deuel was a child survivor whose Lithuanian parents and grandparents were murdered, and who came to Israel through Youth Aliyah. Her paintings express the fears that haunt her.

Survivor guilt

Holocaust survivors have a clear sense that they survived by chance, not because they were better people than those who died. This often produces strong feelings of guilt simply for being alive. Some also feel guilt that they were not able to save their loved ones. Yehudah Bacon from Czechoslovakia survived the Holocaust but his father did not. His drawing shows his father's face in the smoke rising from a crematorium.

A few survivors have been reunited with their loved ones after decades. Some survivors continue to search, using websites and databases in Holocaust museums.

Missing identity

Survivors often had difficulty tracing their relatives. This girl was among many whose photos were published in newspapers in the hope that someone might recognize them. On Israeli radio there were daily broadcasts of the names and details of missing persons. Children who discovered they were orphans also wanted to find out more about who they were.

The second generation

Children of survivors have a deep need to understand their parents' past. Both parents of the American artist Art Spiegelman were survivors. He explored their experiences in a graphic novel, called *Maus*, in which the perpetrators were cats and the victims mice.

VOICES
SURVIVORS LOOK BACK

In spite of the millions who died, many of those who survived the darkest hours of the Holocaust went on to live full lives around the world. However, such cruelty and suffering is unforgettable, and for most of these survivors one question that remains in their minds today is "Why did this happen?"

"I'VE GOT THREE children — two boys and a girl...I'm very happy, very proud. So there you are, out of where I was — to come to this! It's my greatest joy. So God was good to me... With all the troubles that I've had in life, this makes up for it because I've got a wonderful life with my family and that's all that counts... What the Germans did to us — I can't forget, I can't forget. I can't for the life of me understand how it could have happened. I can not understand, I don't know, I just don't know."

"I CAN'T BLAME all the Germans and the young generations — how can I say it's their fault? I can't! But I've never been back to Germany since then, since I left it. I do want to before I die, I do want to go back. And my sister wants to go back to Auschwitz to say Kaddish for my parents and my brothers and sister because that's where they died. But other than that I have no interest to go back to Germany and the other places. I have no desire to go back. None whatsoever."

Peter Hersch
(Born in Czechoslovakia, 1930)
Peter struggles to understand why the Holocaust happened and expresses his love for his family.

"MY CHILDREN WANTED to know about the number on my arm and naturally they were talking about what happened to the Jews because they wanted to know, 'Where is Grandma and Grandpa?' So I told them just in a capsule way what happened to us. I explained to them where I came from and all that but nothing in detail."

"I HAVE TO convince myself that there is a reason for everything. Because otherwise I would say,'Why did God give the strength to Hitler, to commit this murder act, to annihilate six million Jews and others at the same time? Why was he granted that power since he was an evil man? Why?' That answer nobody can give me."

"PEOPLE CAME to these wires when they could not bear anymore the suffering and the hunger and the starvation. Every morning you could see people hanging from these wires committing suicide, ending their lives. I'm looking at these today and it's hard to believe — if these poles could tell the stories of the things that happened here. It couldn't be true, we keep saying to ourselves, it couldn't be true. Yet we all are marked, we all have the numbers on our arms which tells us that, yes, we were here... I learned something here but I wonder whether the world learned anything. The way you look around the world today you wonder — what did we learn from the Holocaust? What did we learn from this place?... Look at this place. Look at the size of it! Can you imagine the millions that perished here?"

Diana Golden
(Born in Greece, 1922)
After the war, Diana emigrated to the United States. Like many other survivors, she wonders how the Holocaust happened.

Renée Firestone
(Born in Czechoslovakia, 1924)
Many years after she emigrated to the United States, Renée returned to Auschwitz to visit the memorial site.

WAR CRIMES TRIALS

THE ALLIES WERE COMMITTED to bringing Nazis to justice without delay and trials began soon after the end of the war. The early trials were limited in what they could do and only involved the highest-ranking Nazis. While some Nazis surrendered, others committed suicide. A large number fled and escaped justice. Individuals and organizations known as "Nazi hunters" still actively seek out Nazis to bring to trial.

Hitler's death
Hitler's suicide just days before the end of World War II was a major news item on the radio and in newspapers all around the globe. The American weekly magazine *Time* featured this strong image on its front cover.

HIMMLER
Heinrich Himmler, the man behind the Final Solution, was convinced Germany should seek peace with Britain and America. Discovering this, Hitler ordered his arrest. Himmler escaped in disguise but was arrested by the British and committed suicide before he could be interrogated.

GOEBBELS
After Hitler's suicide, Joseph Goebbels, Minister for Propaganda, remained in the bunker. He and his wife resolved to die along with their six children. A doctor gave the children lethal injections. Then Goebbels ordered SS orderlies to shoot him and his wife.

BORMANN
On 30 April 1945, after Hitler's suicide, his powerful private secretary Martin Bormann left the bunker and disappeared. He was sentenced to death *in absentia* at Nuremberg. A body was later found in Berlin and Bormann was pronounced dead by a German court in 1973.

Death and disappearance
In January 1945, Hitler made his new headquarters in a bunker in Berlin. As the war drew to a close, he realized Germany would be defeated. On 30 April 1945, he took his own life, along with Eva Braun whom he had married the previous day. This table shows what happened to other senior Nazis.

The Belsen trials
British forces took control of Bergen-Belsen and conducted trials of the most senior Nazis there. Here, they are arresting the camp commander, Josef Kramer. Trials of 44 Nazis took place in November 1945, for crimes committed at both Belsen and Auschwitz. Thirty were found guilty and given sentences ranging from one year in prison to death.

International Military Tribunal
By August 1945, the Allies agreed to hold an International Military Tribunal. The tribunal would be based on "natural justice" because several countries were involved, each with different law codes. The charges included war crimes and crimes against humanity, and the Nazis could not defend themselves by saying that they were simply obeying orders. Many, many documents had to be sorted.

The Nuremberg trials

As Berlin was war-damaged, the trials took place
in Nuremberg, a city with symbolic significance as
the place where racial laws had been passed. Both
Nazi policy and the actions of individuals were tried.
There were 22 defendants, some of whom are pictured
here. Three were acquitted, seven were given life
imprisonment, and 12 received death sentences.

"Justice in Jerusalem"

Adolf Eichmann, responsible for the
mass transports to death camps, fled to
Argentina. In 1960 he was captured by
the Israeli Secret Service and brought to
Jerusalem, Israel, for trial (left). He was
found guilty of war crimes and crimes
against humanity, and was hanged.

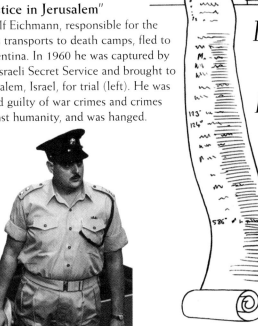

*Between 1945 and 1985,
about 5,000 convicted
Nazi war criminals were
executed and 10,000
imprisoned.*

The Butcher of Lyons

Klaus Barbie, the head of the Gestapo in
Lyons, France, was tracked down by
Nazi hunters. His trial concentrated on
his part in the Final Solution. The long
scroll in this cartoon reads, "List of
people murdered or deported". In 1987
he was sentenced to life imprisonment.

VOICES
NAZIS ON TRIAL

Many of those on trial denied responsibility for their actions – claiming they were simply following orders. A few admitted their crimes but remained defiant, saying they regretted nothing. Here, prosecutors recall their experiences at the trial, while comments from Rudolf Hoess and Josef Kramer at the time of their trials illustrate the chilling single-mindedness of the Nazis.

I WAS WORKING on the main trial against the Nazi government. I saw all those members of the Nazi government. One man that did impress me was Goering. He was quite deflated but he is the only one who had the guts to recognise his crimes. He talked for two days in his defence and he said, 'If I have to start all over again I would do the same thing because I did it for the greatness of my people.' All the others were saying, 'Well, we followed the orders of our Führer. We didn't have our wills so we are innocent.' In fact Ribbentrop went even so far when he was asked, 'Did you find that concentration camp that was on the outskirts of Berlin?' He says 'No, that's not a concentration camp. That was a home for retired Jews.'

I HAD NO feelings in carrying out these things, because I received an order. That, incidentally, is the way I was trained.

Josef Kramer
The commandant of Belsen, Kramer comments on his attitude towards the atrocities he carried out.

Demetrius Dvoichenko-Markov
A sergeant in US Army during the war, Demetrius later worked as research analyst collating evidence for the prosecution at Nuremberg.

"NONE OF THE defendants pleaded guilty initially. Later on, some confessed to a considerable amount of guilt. Like Frank, the 'Gauleiter', the Commander of Poland, he said, 'A thousand years will go by and the guilt of the German people will not be erased.' He had a feeling of something not being right. But he didn't have the guts while the war was going on… when he was standing before his judges he regretted what he had done and what the others had done. They didn't have much power. Power was concentrated in Hitler, Himmler, Goering, and Goebbels. Hitler was dead, Himmler committed suicide in Hamburg when he was caught by the British, and Goebbels committed suicide on May 1st in the chancery in Berlin, killing his six children and his wife and himself. The people in the dock in Nuremberg blamed it all on them, they were safely dead so they were beyond the power of the Allies to do anything. 'Did you do this?' 'No, I didn't, Goebbels did it.' We can't cross-examine Goebbels. That was their trick. I read the German press in those days, whatever there was — controlled press — and most people were quite satisfied with the judgment. They found it fair that they were not just summarily executed."

"WHEN I STAND before you here, Judges of Israel, to lead the Prosecution of Adolf Eichmann, I am not standing alone. With me are six million accusers. But they cannot rise to their feet and point an accusing finger towards him who sits in the dock and cry: 'I accuse.' For their ashes are piled up on the hills of Auschwitz and the fields of Treblinka, and are strewn in the forests of Poland. Their graves are scattered throughout the length and breadth of Europe. Their blood cries out, but their voice is not heard. Therefore I will be their spokesman and in their name I will unfold the awesome indictment."

"AT AUSCHWITZ, I used Zyklon B, which was a crystallized prussic acid which we dropped into the death chamber from a small opening. It took from 3 to 15 minutes to kill the people in the death chamber, depending on the climatic conditions. We knew the people were dead because their screaming stopped."

Rudolf Hoess,
Hoess describes without emotion the process of killing victims using Zykoln B gas during his trial at Nuremberg.

Peter Less
Peter fled to Switzerland in 1938. His parents were killed in Auschwitz. He later worked as an interpreter at Nuremberg.

Gideon Hausner
The Israeli attorney general, Gideon Hausner, was the chief prosecutor at the trial of Adolf Eichmann in 1961.

STOLEN PROPERTY AND COMPENSATION

WHEN THE NAZIS deported their victims, they seized their valuables or took them as payment for exit visas. Since the Holocaust, survivors and organizations acting on their behalf have made attempts at compensation from Germany, other governments, banks, and industries. They are not so much motivated by the money involved but by a desire for the suffering to be recognized and for the perpetrators to admit their guilt.

Killing people; saving art

Hitler wanted national collections of art to support Nazi belief in German supremacy and strengthen the appearance of power. He was against modern art and art on Jewish themes, which he called "degenerate", such as this collection in Berlin. Many works of art were destroyed, but very famous works were sold.

Nazi loot

When the Nazis stole valuables from their victims, they protected them from bombs by storing them in caves, vaults, and cellars. As American and British troops entered Germany, they discovered hoards of jewellery, rare books, and priceless works of art. This American soldier is guarding bars of gold.

In 1951, Chancellor Adenauer admitted German responsibility for "unspeakable crimes" and "infinite suffering", and reparations as a "measure of justice".

The gold train

This Nazi "gold train" was carrying $200 million of gold, art, and valuables taken from Hungarian Jews, when American troops captured it in May 1945. They seized the loot thinking it was enemy property. A group of Hungarian survivors later demanded compensation from the US government, who claimed not to have known that the valuables belonged to victims. The US settled with 32 Hungarian survivors in 2004.

Swiss bank accounts

Although many killed in the Holocaust had opened bank accounts in neutral Switzerland, the banks refused to release the money to relatives without the correct paperwork. The Nazis did not issue death certificates and the bank documents were lost. Facing charges of corruption and under pressure to release the money, the Swiss banks donated large sums to charity. In 1997, they finally allowed access to the bank records. Here, a survivor is completing paperwork to access bank records.

Romany claim against IBM

Material published in 2001 alleged that IBM, an American computer company, had developed punch-card technology to make the selection of Holocaust victims more efficient. A Romany organization planned to sue IBM for its role, claiming $10,000 per Romany orphan. This would be a major step for Romanies seeking recognition of their loss. So far, no action has been taken.

Claims conference

The Conference on Jewish Material Claims Against Germany was set up in 1951. It negotiated claims, distributed money to the neediest survivors and their heirs, and recovered unclaimed German Jewish property. West German Chancellor Adenauer is shown signing the reparation agreement.

"Blood money"

In 1952, Israel and Germany entered discussions about reparations. Some in Israel felt that payment from Germany would be "blood money", or money taken in return for lives. Others thought money was needed by the survivors and Germany should pay for its crimes. Germany haggled over the sum, beating Israel down to half. They did not pay in cash, but in German goods, like this ship. Many Israelis resented German goods, as they were a reminder of the Holocaust.

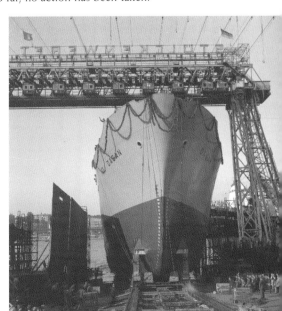

THE SITES OF THE CAMPS TODAY

VERY LITTLE REMAINS OF MOST CAMPS, which were deliberately demolished or left to decay over time. As the map of Europe changes, so do the politics of the places where the camps stand and opinions on how the sites should be managed. There are strong feelings about how some groups stamp their religious or political mark on both the camps and the memory of those who perished. Auschwitz is now a World Heritage Site and in 2006 the Polish government asked for it to be called "Former Nazi German Concentration Camp of Auschwitz".

Pilgrim or tourist?
Former concentration camps, especially Auschwitz in Poland, attract a large number of visitors. Some come as pilgrims, some as students, and some as tourists. Visitors are sometimes horrified that Auschwitz has become so commercialized, and even has hot-dog stands outside. For some, the presence of large crowds of noisy people is insensitive. Visitors often pose to have their photo taken here, under the famous *Arbeit Macht Frei* (Work Brings Freedom) sign.

The "railway" at Treblinka
In 1943, the Nazis destroyed the camp and railway line at Treblinka in Poland. However, after the Holocaust, Soviet authorities erected a huge slab saying "Never Again" in many languages. There are also hundreds of standing stones, representing a town or city which was once home to the victims, and the symbolic blocks (above) mark the path of the railway.

As it was
A few camps were not destroyed by the Nazis or the Allies. At Auschwitz and Majdanek, some barracks, gas chambers, crematoria, and other buildings are still standing. They give some insight into the nature of daily life in the camps, such as the sleeping arrangements in this barrack at Majdanek. But the wooden barracks are slowly rotting away and will eventually fall apart.

More than half a million people visit the site of the former concentration camp at Auschwitz every year.

Human remains

The sites of the concentration camps are effectively huge cemeteries, where the remains of an unknown and mostly nameless number of people lie. To visit a camp is to step on invisible graves. In some camps, ashes have been gathered together and marked. This mausoleum at Majdanek in Poland contains ashes from the nearby crematorium. The Polish inscription reads "Let our fate be a warning for you".

Crosses at Auschwitz

The first Christian crosses appeared at Auschwitz-Birkenau in 1979, when the Polish Pope, John Paul II, celebrated Mass there. In 1988, nuns placed the first of many crosses at Auschwitz I, where they had converted the building formerly used to store Zyklon B gas into a convent. Jewish groups protested against the crosses and the location of the convent. In 1993 the nuns left, but the crosses still remain.

Soviet influences

When Poland was a communist country, Soviet influences on political life were very strong. The Soviet Union was proud of the defeat of Nazism and erected many monuments, like this one at the former labour camp of Plaszow in Poland. They were usually huge slabs that symbolized Soviet power. Memorial markers referred to the "victims of fascism", but not to Jews or Romanies.

Memorial stones

All former concentration camps have plaques or markers, and most also display sculptures or installations commemorating the dead. In some camps there are natural stones placed as symbolic gravestones at the spot of a mass grave. Here, at Buchenwald in Germany, the names of the camps where Nazis murdered Romanies are carved into some of the stones. They include Buchenwald itself.

MEMORIALS, MUSEUMS, EDUCATION

IN MANY PARTS OF THE WORLD, especially in Europe, North America, and Israel, sculptures and installations have been erected to commemorate the Holocaust. They capture the experience of the Holocaust, remember the lives lost, and prompt lessons to be learned from it. Educational programmes and study units enable children and adults to understand what happened and why – in the hope that such events will never happen again.

Holocaust Memorial Day
Some countries commemorate the Holocaust with civic ceremonies and educational programmes. In Israel, the date of Holocaust and Heroism Memorial Day coincides with that of the Warsaw Ghetto Uprising. Places of entertainment are closed and people stand silent and still for two minutes wherever they happen to be.

Holocaust artefacts as memorials
Using authentic artefacts from the Holocaust makes memory very immediate and enables those viewing them to feel empathy. This "Memorial to the Deportees" at Yad Vashem, in Jerusalem, Israel, is an actual train used in the deportations. The broken tracks symbolize the deaths of the victims and also the end of the Holocaust.

Memorial sculptures and installations
Some Holocaust memorials express pain and tragedy, while some focus on the idea of new life and hope. Others, such as this memorial of 2,700 different-sized coffin-like stone blocks, created in Berlin in 2005, enable people to reflect as they walk between them.

Liberty and liberation

In the USA, the Holocaust is linked to America's role in the defeat of Nazism and as liberators of the camps. This "Liberation Monument" created by Nathan Rappaport expresses the idea of America as the "land of the free". It stands in New York Harbor, a short distance from the Statue of Liberty.

"Righteous among the Nations"

Yad Vashem, the Holocaust museum and memorial centre in Jerusalem, honours non-Jews who risked their lives to help Jews by hiding them or helping them to escape. It calls them "Righteous among the Nations" and has planted trees in their names in this Avenue of the Righteous. Yad Vashem also honours them in person, with a special ceremony and medal.

HOLOCAUST TERMS

Holocaust – an ancient Greek term meaning "totally burned sacrifice" – now refers to the mass murder of Jews by the Nazis during World War II

Porrajmos – "devouring" – a term that was coined by the Romany people to describe the Holocaust

Sho'ah – "catastrophe" – a Hebrew word from the Bible, used by Jews for the Holocaust

Hurban – "destruction" – another Hebrew word for the Holocaust, less commonly used than *Sho'ah*

Israel has recognized more than 20,000 people as "Righteous among the Nations" for risking their lives to save Jews.

Education

Holocaust museums play a large part in educating the public, and children in Israel, Germany, and the USA learn about the Holocaust at school. This image – expressing empathy for a child victim denied the joys of childhood – was created by a young artist at Long Island High School, USA, as part of a programme by the Holocaust Resource Center.

STORIES OF THE SURVIVORS

Alexander Van Kollem

Born in 1928 in Amsterdam, the Netherlands, Alexander's family was interned in Vught transit camp in 1941. His father's boss got the family back to Amsterdam, where they went into hiding. He was liberated from the last hiding place by the British in May 1945, but both his parents died at Auschwitz. After the war he returned to Amsterdam before emigrating to the USA, where he married in 1952.

Aniela Ania Radek

Born in Poland in 1926, Aniela is a Roman Catholic. In 1941 she was sent to Auschwitz in Poland. After escaping, she went into hiding in a farmhouse near Augsberg. Meanwhile, her father had been killed in France for criticizing the communists. Aniela went to the Sorbonne in France and later to university in Montreal, Canada. She married in Toronto in 1954 and has one daughter.

Bernard Shuster

Born in Poland in 1928, Bernard's father died before the war and his mother was shot trying to escape from one of the ghettos. Bernard went into hiding and was later liberated by the Russians from the woods near Jasionowka in Poland. He went into Santa Cesarea Displaced Persons camp in Italy from 1945–47 before emigrating to New York. He studied law at Harvard and works with the US Jewish community.

Eric Richmond

Born in Vienna in 1924, Eric fled Austria in 1938 as part of the *Kindertransport* and came to England. During the war he made army boots and years later become a restaurateur and hotelier. In 1970 he went back to visit Austria, but only very briefly. His father and mother were both killed during the war. He married in Germany in 1963 and has one daughter. He now lives in England.

Felicia Carmelly

Born in Romania in 1931, Felicia was sent to Shargorod ghetto in Transnistria, Ukraine, in 1941 where she worked in the fields until 1944. She was liberated by the Soviet army in 1945 and returned to Romania before emigrating to Canada. She has one daughter. Felicia went on to gain a PhD in Psychology and to publish a book. She is the founder of the Transnistria Survivors Association of Toronto.

Fred Spiegel

Born in Germany in 1932, Fred's mother emigrated to England in the hope of sending for Fred and his sister later. However, war broke out and Fred was sent to Bergen-Belsen, via Westerbork, and was eventually liberated by the Americans. After the war he travelled to England, Chile, Israel, and the USA. His mother and sister survived the war. Fred is married with three children.

The people who are quoted throughout the book on the Voices spreads are introduced on these pages. Their incredible stories of strength and survival provide a moving testimony to the power of the human spirit.

Claire Boren
Born in Poland in 1938, Claire and her family were sent to Mizoch ghetto in 1942, and then went into hiding. Initially, she was hidden in an attic. Later, helped by a Baptist farmer, she and her mother hid in a hole beneath a pigsty for three months. She was liberated by the Soviet army in early 1944. She then went to Eshwege Displaced Persons camp from 1946–49 before emigrating to the USA.

Diana Golden
Born in 1922 on the Greek island of Rhodes, Diana and her family were transported to a concentration camp near Athens in 1944, after the Germans occupied the island. The family was then sent to Auschwitz. Her father died on the journey and she never saw her mother again. She was later sent to Terezin, where she was liberated by the Soviets. After the war Diana started a new life in the USA.

Emma Mogilensky
Born in Germany in 1923, Emma fled in 1939 and caught a train to London where she joined the British Army, working as a cook. In 1950 she emigrated to the USA, where she met her husband. In 1992 she visited her home town of Cronheim in Germany. Both her parents were killed in the Holocaust but her brother escaped and now also lives in the USA. She has three children.

Henry Greenblatt
Born in Poland in 1930, Henry's parents and sister were killed in 1942. He spent time in the Warsaw ghetto before moving to Siedlce ghetto. In 1942, on a death march from Siedlce, he managed to escape and went into hiding under a false identity, working on a farm from 1943–46, and as part of the resistance for the Home Army of Poland. Henry now lives in the USA.

Henry Oster
Born in 1928 in Germany, Henry and his family were deported to Łódź ghetto in Poland in 1941, where Henry's father died of malnutrition. In 1943, Henry and his mother were deported to Auschwitz where he was separated from his mother whom he never saw again. At the end of 1944, he was sent on a death march to Buchenwald where he remained until liberation by the Americans in 1945.

Julia Lentini
Born in 1926 in Biedenkopf, Germany, to a Romany family, Julia and her family were arrested in 1943 and sent to Auschwitz, where both her parents died. She was moved to Schlieben camp in 1945 where she was later liberated by the Soviets. After the war she was housed as a war refugee near Biedenkopf. She later met and married an American soldier and they emigrated to the USA in 1946.

STORIES OF THE SURVIVORS

Leonie Hilton

Leonie was born in Germany in 1916. Although her mother was Jewish, Leonie was brought up as a Christian by her father and stepmother, and didn't realize that she was Jewish until Hitler came to power and introduced his racist laws. Her first husband died as a prisoner of war in Singapore. She has one son, and emigrated to Australia in 1943 where she has lived ever since.

Lola Putt

Born in Greece in 1926, Lola was sent to a ghetto in 1943. After one week she was taken to Auschwitz, and later to Birkenau. In the camps she had to dig graves and remove valuables from victims. She was sent on a death march in 1945 from Poland and liberated by the Soviets and Americans after two days on the march. Lola's father, mother, and three of her siblings died in Auschwitz. She lives in Australia.

Mayer Schondorf

Born in 1928 in Czechoslovakia, Mayer and his family were deported to the Nové Mesto internment camp. They later went to Auschwitz where the family was separated. In 1945, he went on a death march to Gross Rosen concentration camp, and shortly after to Buchenwald. He was liberated by the Americans, and later reunited with his mother, brother, and sister. He married another survivor and lives in Canada.

Renée Firestone

Born in Czechoslovakia in 1924, Renée and her family were deported to Auschwitz in 1944, where her mother and sister were killed. Her brother escaped and joined the partisans. Renée was later transferred to Liebau camp in Germany to work in a munitions factory. She was liberated by the Soviets and later reunited with her brother and father. She married another survivor and lives in the USA.

Rose Silberberg-Skier

Born in 1934 in Poland, Rose's family briefly went into hiding in 1942, but were caught and sent to Srodula ghetto in 1943. Rose escaped the ghetto with her aunt. They were later given German papers by the resistance and went to Germany where they found work in a convent until liberation by the Soviets in 1945. None of Rose's family survived. She emigrated to the USA in 1951 and is married with three children.

Sigi Hart

Born in Berlin in 1925, Sigi and his family fled to Belgium in 1938. They spent the next few years in France trying to avoid capture. When Italy surrendered in 1943, Sigi went to Florence but was captured and sent to Auschwitz. He was moved to Nordhausen and then to Bergen-Belsen, but was liberated one month later by the British. He moved to Tel Aviv in Israel where he married in 1953. In 1957 the whole family emigrated to the USA.

Michelle Cohen-Rodriguez

Born in 1935 in Paris, Michelle and her family went into hiding in Paris in 1940. Two of her brothers joined the Maquis resistance organization and, when Michelle was sent to Drancy camp, her brother Abel, dressed as a German soldier, helped her to escape. She was hidden in a convent, but later placed with a foster family until the end of the war. After liberation, Michelle initially returned to Paris, but emigrated to the USA in 1955 where she married and had one child.

Peter Hersch

Born in Czechoslovakia in 1930, Peter and his family were deported to the Mukacevo ghetto in 1944. The family were then sent to Auschwitz, where his mother and three siblings were killed. His father also did not survive, and Peter was sent to Mauthausen. He was later in Gusen camp and in 1945 was sent on a death march to Gunskirchen camp, which was liberated by the Americans. After the war, Peter travelled around Romania and Hungary, searching for relatives. In 1948 he emigrated to Australia and married.

Thea Rumstein

Born in Vienna in 1928, Thea's family was deported to Terezin in 1942. In 1944, the family was sent to Auschwitz, where her father was killed. Thea and her mother then went to Freiberg camp in Germany before being transferred to Mauthausen. They were liberated by the Americans. After the war, Thea and her mother returned to Vienna where she briefly worked for the American Jewish Joint Distribution Committee and was reunited with her brother. She now lives in the USA.

Vera Eden

Born in Prague in 1930, Vera was initially in Terezin ghetto, before being sent to Auschwitz from 1942–44. Her father died at Auschwitz and her mother at Bergen-Belsen. Her sister survived. Later, Vera was moved to Kurzbach camp for a year and then to Gross Rosen concentration camp. She was liberated by the British from Bergen-Belsen in 1945. She returned to Prague, where she married before joining the army in Israel from 1950–52. She now lives in Canada.

Vera Gissing

Born in Prague in 1928, Vera's parents sent her and her sister to England on the *Kinderstransport* in 1939 to escape the Holocaust. Vera was sent to a family in Liverpool. Her foster parents sent her to the Czech school in Wales, which is where she was when she heard the war was over. Her father died on a death march in Poland and her mother died at Bergen-Belsen. Her sister now lives in New Zealand. Vera married in 1949 and has three children. She still lives in England.

BIG QUESTIONS

LEARNING ABOUT THE HOLOCAUST answers many questions, but many more remain ... Can someone who did wrong really say, "I was only obeying orders"? Should we judge how people behaved in the Holocaust, such as the victims who did not resist the Nazis or people who did not help? What about buying goods from "Nazi" companies or using medicines developed by Nazi doctors? Should we forgive? Can we forget? What can we do so that nothing like the Holocaust ever happens again?

Survivors speak
At first, very few Holocaust survivors could talk about their suffering, especially to strangers. But when they heard people denying that the Holocaust happened, many of them felt they had to speak out. A school in Tennessee, USA, invited this survivor to speak to the children. The children discovered that meeting and learning about one person is more valuable than learning facts about millions.

The churches and the Holocaust
Although there are churches that still preach traditional beliefs about Jews, some have revised their views. Jewish-Christian relations are now closer than in recent decades. In 2006, Pope Benedict XVI visited Auschwitz (left). The previous Pope, John Paul II, also visited the camp, and apologized for the fact that Christian beliefs had caused Jewish suffering.

Holocaust denial
Despite the facts about the Holocaust, there are still anti-Semitic individuals and groups who claim that it never happened, or that it has been exaggerated. In Britain in 2000, Holocaust denier David Irving lost his court case against historian Deborah Lipstadt (above) and her publishing company, in which he accused them of libel (slander).

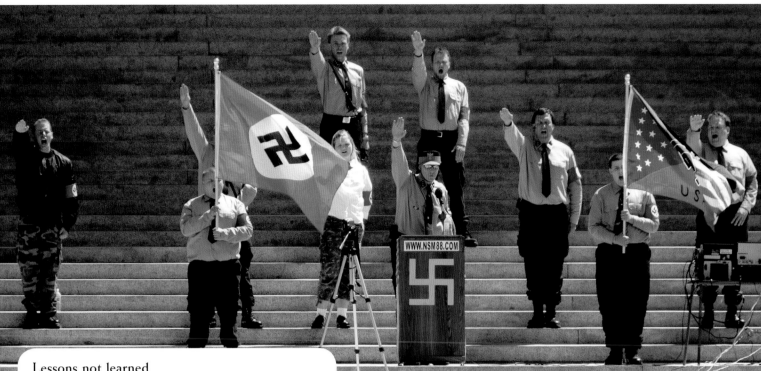

Lessons not learned

More than 60 years after the Holocaust, nothing has happened on quite the same scale. Yet there is still rampant racism and acts of genocide in many parts of the world. In Europe and North America neo (new) Nazi groups adopt the language and the style of the Nazis, as in this demonstration in Olympia, Washington, USA.

Never again

The horrors of the Holocaust make many individuals and groups determined to work for a more loving and peaceful world, and to prevent any further genocide. In addition, some Jewish individuals and groups realize that there is a need to defend the Jewish community. The slogan on this girl's T-shirt – Never Again – affirms the commitment to stop anything like the Holocaust ever happening again.

Making good again

Not all Nazis were German. Not all Germans were Nazis. Germany has repealed Nazi laws and changed Nazi political and social systems in a process called de-Nazification. It has also made moves to put right what it did wrong through various projects. Many young Germans feel responsible for what their country did. This group is part of a project to restore Jewish cemeteries in Eastern Europe.

Voices from the past

In 1942, 14-year-old Petr Gens was deported to Theresienstadt. He was interested in astronomy and science, and also liked art. His drawing *Moon Landscape* shows his view of Earth from the cratered moon. He drew the Earth as the moon appears to us – peaceful and full of light. In 1944, Petr was murdered at Auschwitz. His drawing survives to challenge and inspire us.

"I have tried to keep memory alive … I have tried to fight those who would forget. Because if we forget, we are guilty, we are accomplices."

Elie Wiesel, Nobel Prize speech, 1986

The forest of steles (slabs of stone) at the entrance to the Hall of Murdered Children, at Israel's national Holocaust memorial, Yad Vashem

Allies
The nations that joined with Britain to fight Nazi Germany during World War II, including the Soviet Union, the USA, and France.

Annex
To add new land to existing territory.

Anschluss
Term used to describe the German takeover of Austria in 1938, from the German word meaning "join".

Anti-Semitism
A form of racism based on hatred of, and prejudice against, Jews.

Aryan
The term the Nazis used to describe people who they believed were of pure German blood – a superior race of white people, with blond hair and blue eyes.

Axis Powers
Name given to the alliance of Germany and Italy, and later Japan, during World War II.

Blitzkreig
German for "lightning war" – an intense military campaign intended to bring swift results. The term "The Blitz" was used to describe German air raids on London in 1940–41.

Communism
The political theory that advocates a society in which all property is publicly owned and each person is paid according to his or her needs. A supporter is known as a communist.

Concentration camp
A prison camp set up for holding large numbers of political prisoners.

Crematorium
A building with large ovens for burning dead bodies.

Czechoslovakia
Until 1993, the two nations now known as the Czech Republic and Slovakia were united as the country of Czechoslovakia. Between 1939 and 1945, Czechoslovakia was split into Bohemia and Moravia, and Slovakia.

Death camp
A camp set up to exterminate inmates quickly and efficiently.

Displaced Person (DP)
A person who is left with no country to go to after a war.

Einsatzgruppen
Nazi mobile killing squads, set up by the SS to follow the German army as they conquered land in Eastern Europe, and round up and kill Jews.

Emancipation
A period of freedom from traditional ideas, also the state of being free from restrictions or control.

Enlightenment
The 18th-century European philosophy emphasizing reason and individualism rather than tradition.

Fascism
A system of strong government by a leader with powerful appeal, who is dedicated to the rebirth of a nation. A supporter is known as a Fascist.

Final Solution
The Nazi term for the plan to exterminate the Jews of Europe – the solution to what they believed was the "Jewish problem".

Führer
The German word meaning "leader" applied to Hitler.

General Government
The name given to the areas of Poland occupied by Germany in 1939, but not incorporated into the Third Reich.

Genocide
The deliberate attempt to destroy a national, religious, racial, or ethnic group, in whole or in part.

Gentile
A person who is not Jewish.

Gestapo
The secret police of Nazi Germany.

Ghetto
An area of a city where Jews were forced to live in cramped, inhumane conditions during Nazi rule.

Hebrew
The language spoken in Israel today. Also, the name for a member of the tribe that originated in ancient Palestine.

Holocaust
The mass murder of the Jews, and other minorities, by the Nazis between 1933 and 1945.

Israel
The modern Jewish state in the Middle East, established in 1948. The "Land of Israel" is also the traditional name for the ancient Hebrew nation (c. 930–721 BCE).

Judenrat
A Jewish council set up by the Nazis to run ghetto communities during World War II.

Kapo
A concentration camp prisoner who supervised other prisoners, for which he or she received privileges.

Kindertransport
The mass evacuation of children from Germany to Britain in 1938.

Kristallnacht
From the German, meaning "Night of Broken Glass", the night of violence against Jews and Jewish property on 9–10 November, 1938.

Labour camp
A prison camp in which inmates are subjected to enforced hard labour.

Middle Ages
The period of European history between the 5th and 15th centuries. Also known as the medieval period.

Nazi Party
The National Socialist German Workers' Party, led by Hitler. The Party believed in strong military leadership to enforce nationalistic, racist, and anti-Semitic policies.

Palestine
Traditionally, the area of the Middle East that once included the countries now called Israel and Jordan. Today, Palestine is made up of areas of the West Bank and Gaza.

Partisan
A resistance fighter operating behind enemy lines.

Pogrom
An organized, often officially encouraged, attack on a minority group.

Propaganda
Information – sometimes false or partly false – used to influence the opinions of others.

Putsch
A sudden attempt at political revolution or a violent uprising, from the German word for "thrust" or "blow".

Reichstag
The German Parliament.

Reparations
To make amends for a wrongdoing, and also the payment of compensation by a defeated nation for war damages.

Republic
A state in which power is held by the people or their elected representatives, not by a monarch.

Revolution
The overthrow of a government or social order by force.

Romany
The name for a nomadic group of people, often referred to by the derogatory term of "Gypsies".

Shtetl
A small Jewish town or village in Eastern Europe or Russia.

Sinti
A nomadic people of Europe, closely related to the Romany.

Social democracy
The political belief in moving gradually and peacefully to a system of socialism (state ownership) by democratic (system of free elections) means. A supporter is known as a social democrat.

Sonderkommando
Prisoners of death camps who were forced to remove dead bodies in the gas chambers for cremation or burial. From the German word *sonder*, meaning "special".

Soviet Union
The name given to the Russian Empire after the revolution of 1917, and short for the Union of Soviet Socialist Republics (USSR). In 1991, when the Soviet Union collapsed, the area became known as the Commonwealth of Independent States (CIS).

SS
From the German *Schutzstaffel*, meaning "protective squad". The SS began as Hitler's personal guard but grew to become a large and powerful organization responsible for concentration camps and racial matters.

Storm troopers
Also known as Brownshirts, a force of troops used by the Nazi party to help Hitler rise to power.

Synagogue
A building used for Jewish religious study, worship, and celebration.

Third Reich
The period of German government from 1933–45, from the German meaning "Third Empire".

Torah
The Jewish sacred writings, used in synagogues in the form of scrolls.

Transit camp
A camp where inmates are held temporarily before being moved on.

USSR (see Soviet Union)

Vichy France
The area of southern France occupied by Germany between 1942 and 1945.

Yiddish
The traditional language of the Jews of Eastern Europe, based on German, Hebrew, and several modern languages including Polish and Russian.

Zionism
The movement for the re-establishment and the development of a Jewish nation in the area that is now Israel.

GLOSSARY

INDEX

INDEX

CREDITS

The publisher would like to thank the following for their kind permission to reproduce their photographs:

(Key: a-above; b-below/bottom; c-centre; f-far; l-left; r-right; t-top)

1 akg-images: Ullstein Bild. 2-3 PunchStock: Stockbyte Platinum. 4-5 akg-images: Juergen Raible. 8-9 Mary Evans Picture Library: (t). 10 akg-images: (cr); Erich Lessing (tl). The Bridgeman Art Library: Index, Forum, Rome, Italy (b). 11 The Art Archive: Galleria Degli Uffizi, Florence/Dagli Orti (br). The Bridgeman Art Library: Private Collection (tl). Angela Gluck Wood: (cr). Zev Radovan/wwwBibleLandPictures.com: (bl). 12 Corbis: Peter M Wilson (tr). Courtesy Barbara Mendes: (cl). Alliance Israelite Universelle: (br). Jorge Vismara: (bl). 13 Alamy Images: Orit Allush (b). DK Images: (t). 14 akg-images: (r); Erich Lessing (tl). 15 Angela Gluck Wood: (bl) (cr). Photo D. Le Neve: (cl). 16 The Bridgeman Art Library: Gift of Sam and Ayala Zacks, 1970, Art Gallery of Ontario, Toronto, Canada. © ADAGP, Paris and DACS, London 2007 (t). 17 akg-images: (bl); Ullstein Bild (cla); United Artists/Album (c). Corbis: David Katzenstein (br). Angela Gluck Wood: (tr). 20 akg-images: (cr); János Kalmár (br); Erich Lessing (tl). ArenaPAL: Marilyn Kingwill (bl). 21 akg-images: (cl). Beth Hatefutsoth, Photo Archive, Tel Aviv: (br). 22 akg-images: (t); Archiv Klaus Wagenbach (c) (cb). Corbis: Bettmann (r). Leeds Library and Information Services, McKenna Collection: (l). 23 akg-images: (fcr); New York, Solomon R. Guggenheim Museum/Erich Lessing (cl). Lebrecht Music and Arts Photo Library: (cr); Laszlo Vámos/ Hungarian Museum of Photography (fcl). The Bridgeman Art Library: Private Collection, Archives Charmet (tr). The Chassidic Art Institute/© Rosa Kleinman: (tl). Corbis: Bettmann (cr); Vincent Kessler/Reuters (b). 26-27 The Bridgeman Art Library: Bibliotheque Mazarine, Paris, France, Archives Charmet. 28-29 Corbis. 30 akg-images: (t) (bl); Ullstein Bild (b). 30-31 TopFoto: Albert Harlingue/Roger-Viollet (b). 31 akg-images: Ullstein Bild (tr). The Bridgeman Art Library: Private Collection, Archives Charmet (tl). 32 akg-images: (cr); Ullstein Bild (c). Mary Evans Picture Library: (tl) (bl); Private Collection/ The Stapleton Collection (r). The Bridgeman Art Library: Private Collection/ Archives Charmet (br). 34 akg-images: (tl). Corbis: Hulton-Deutsch Collection. 34-35 Corbis. 35 akg-images: Ullstein Bild (tr). Courtesy of Professor Randall Bytwerk: (tl). 36 akg-images: (b). Corbis: Bettmann (tr). Mary Evans Picture Library: (tl). 37 akg-images: (br) (tl). 38-39 akg-images: 42 akg-images: (bl); Erich Lessing (tl). 43 akg-images: (bl); Ullstein Bild (tr). Corbis: Bettmann. 44 akg-images: (l); Archiv Boelte (cr); Ullstein Bild (tr). 45 Mary Evans Picture Library: Weimar Archive (t). United States Holocaust Memorial Museum: Courtesy of Marion Davy (cr) (br) (cb). 46 akg-images: Ullstein Bild (bl). Corbis: Bettmann (br). Hulton-Deutsch Collection (bl). 46-47 akg-images: (t). 47 Mary Evans Picture Library: Weimar Archive (t). United States Holocaust Memorial Museum: Courtesy of Virginius Dabney (tr); Courtesy of John Meyerstein (b). 48-49 akg-images: Hans Asemissen (c). 52 akg-images: (t) (br). United States Holocaust Memorial Museum: Courtesy of Lydia Chagoll (t); Evangelical Archive of Alsterdorf (cr). 53 Corbis: Bettmann (tl). Jehovah's Witnesses, History Archives Department, Germany: (br). Landesarchiv Berlin: (tr). 54 akg-images: (l). 54-55 akg-images: (t). 55 akg-images: Ullstein Bild (bl); Andrew Wyeth (tr). 56-57 United States Holocaust Memorial Museum: Courtesy of Zydowski Instytut Historyczny Instytut Naukowo-Badawczy. 58 The Bridgeman Art Library: Alliance Israelite Universelle, Paris, France/ Archives Charmet (tr). Corbis: Bettmann (b). 59 Alamy Images: Cubo Images srl (tc). Corbis: The Art Archive (tr). Heidelberg University Library: (tl). United States Holocaust Memorial Museum: Courtesy of Leon Jacobson (c). 60-61 The Archive of Modern Conflict: Henryk Ross. 62 akg-images: (t). United States Holocaust Memorial Museum: Courtesy of Gila Flam (b). 63 akg-images: (b). United States Holocaust Memorial Museum: Courtesy of Muzeum Sztuki w Lodzi (tr); Courtesy of Jan Kostanski (tl); Courtesy of Zydowski Instytut Historyczny Instytut Naukowo-Badawczy (b). 64 Corbis: Christel Gerstenberg (t). Imperial War Museum: (b). Courtesy of photo archive, Yad Vashem: (cr) (bl). 65 The Archive of Modern Conflict/Chris Boot Ltd.: (br). United

States Holocaust Memorial Museum: (t). Collection of the Yad Vashem Art Museum, Jerusalem: Pavel Fantl (1903-1945) Story Hour, Terezin Ghetto, 1942-1944 Watercolour on paper Gift of the Prague Committee for Documentation, courtesy of Alisa Shek, Caesarea (bl). Courtesy of photo archive, Yad Vashem: (c). 66 United States Holocaust Memorial Museum: The Disease of Hunger: Clinical Research on Starvation Undertaken in the Warsaw Ghetto in 1942 (bl). 66-67 Courtesy of photo archive, Yad Vashem. 67 Jewish Museum, Prague. Courtesy of photo archive, Yad Vashem: (tl) (br). 70 United States Holocaust Memorial Museum: Courtesy of William Begell (cb); Courtesy of Al Moss (br); Courtesy of Lilli Schischa Tauber (t); Courtesy of Zydowski Instytut Historyczny Instytut Naukowo-Badawczy (bl). 71 (c) Beit Lohamei Haghetaot /The Ghetto Fighters House Museum: (tr). United States Holocaust Memorial Museum: Courtesy of Zydowski Instytut Historyczny Instytut Naukowo-Badawczy (bl). Courtesy of photo archive, Yad Vashem: (cl). 74 United States Holocaust Memorial Museum: Courtesy of Irving Milchberg (bl); Courtesy of Zydowski Instytut Historyczny Instytut Naukowo-Badawczy (br). 75 Angela Gluck Wood: (tr). United States Holocaust Memorial Museum: Courtesy of National Archives and Records Administration, College Park (l) (br); Courtesy of Zydowski Instytut Historyczny Instytut Naukowo-Badawczy (cr). 76 The Jewish Historical Institute, Warsaw: (t) (bl) (br). 77 The Jewish Historical Institute, Warsaw: (b); "Mir Lebengeblibene" (1947), Directed by Nathan Gross. United States Holocaust Memorial Museum: Courtesy of Zydowski Instytut Historyczny Instytut Naukowo-Badawczy (tl) (tc). Courtesy of photo archive, Yad Vashem: (cr). 78-79 Getty Images. 80 akg-images: Ullstein Bild (b). United States Holocaust Memorial Museum: Leopold Page Photograph Collection (cr); Courtesy of Andras Tsagatakis (tl). 81 United States Holocaust Memorial Museum: Courtesy of Library of Congress (tr); Courtesy of KZ Gedenkstaette Dachau (tl); Courtesy of Zydowski Instytut Historyczny Instytut Naukowo-Badawczy (br). Courtesy of photo archive, Yad Vashem: (bl). 83 akg-images: (bl); Courtesy of National Archives and Records Administration, College Park (br). United States Holocaust Memorial Museum: Courtesy of National Archives and Records Administration, College Park (tr); Courtesy of Henry Schwarzbaum (tl). 84 Corbis: Bettmann (bl); Sergei Mikhailovich Prokudin-Gorskii (c). Courtesy of photo archive, Yad Vashem: (br). 85 United States Holocaust Memorial Museum: Courtesy of Julius Schatz (br). Courtesy of photo archive, Yad Vashem: Hessisches Hauptstaatsarchiv (bl). 86-87 akg-images: Ullstein Bild. 88 akg-images: (l) (r). 89 akg-images: Ullstein Bild (bl). © Beit Lohamei Haghetaot/The Ghetto House Museum: (tl). Stadt Koln-Historisches Archiv: photo: Knapstein. United States Holocaust Memorial Museum: Courtesy of David Stoliar (br). Courtesy of photo archive, Yad Vashem: (c). 90 Corbis: Arnd Wiegmann/Reuters (b). United States Holocaust Memorial Museum: Courtesy of Tine Thevenin (c). 92-93 akg-images: Michael Teller. 94 akg-images: (c) (br). 95 akg-images: (tl); Ullstein Bild (br). United States Holocaust Memorial Museum: Courtesy of Matthaeus Pibal (tr). 96 akg-images: Ullstein Bild (tr). Courtesy of CEGES/SOMA: (br). TopFoto: Roger-Viollet (cl). 97 akg-images: (c) (b); Ullstein Bild (tr). 98 Courtesy of photo archive, Yad Vashem: (bl) (br). 99 akg-images: Ullstein Bild (t). Wallstein Verlag: Helga Weissova: Zeichne was Du siehst/Draw what you see. Zeichnungen eines Kindes aus Theresienstadt/Terezin. ed. by Niedersachsischer Verein zur Forderung von Theresienstadt / Terezin e. V. © Wallstein Verlag, Germany 1998. All rights reserved. (br). Courtesy of photo archive, Yad Vashem: (tr). 102 © Alexandre Oler: as published in Witness, Images of Auschwitz with illustrations by David Olère and text by Alexandre Oler, 1998 WESTWIND PRESS (cl). United States Holocaust Memorial Museum: Courtesy of Archiwum Dokumentacji Mechanicznej (t). Courtesy of photo archive, Yad Vashem: (bl) (br). 103 Corbis: Ira Nowinski (br). United States Holocaust Memorial Museum: Prof. Leopold Pfefferberg Collection (tl); Main Commission for the Investigation of Nazi War Crimes (tr); Courtesy of Archiwum Panstwowego Muzeum na Majdanku (bl). 104 akg-images: (cr). © Alexandre Oler: as published in Witness, Images of Auschwitz with illustrations by David Olère and text by Alexandre Oler, 1998 WESTWIND PRESS (br). Collection of the Yad Vashem Art Museum, Jerusalem: Zinovii Tolkatchev (1903-1977) Appell, Majdanek, 1944. Gouache, charcoal and crayon on paper. Gift of Sigmund A. Rolat, New York, in loving memory of his parents, Henryk and Mania, who perished in the Holocaust (c). Courtesy of photo archive, Yad Vashem: (cl). 105 akg-images: (cl); Licensed by DACS, 2007 (bl). Collection of the Yad Vashem Art Museum, Jerusalem: Pavel Fantl (1903-1945) Metamorphosis, Terezin Ghetto,

1944. Watercolour on paper. Gift of the Prague Committee for Documentation, courtesy of Alisa Shek, Caesarea. (t). **Courtesy of photo archive, Yad Vashem:** (br); Yad Vashem Artifacts Collection. Gift of Dr. Gideon N. Levy & Family, Orselina, Switzerland (c). **108** akg-images: Michael Teller (t). TopFoto: (b). **109** akg-images: (tr). Alamy Images: Paul Springett. Auschwitz -Birkenau Memorial & Museum: (cl); Wladyslaw Siwek (tl). **United States Holocaust Memorial Museum:** Courtesy of Frieda Fisz Greenspan (cr); Courtesy of Yad Vashem. (bc); akg-images: Michael Teller (tr). **110-111** akg-images: Ullstein Bild (b). Judy Brody/Graphic Witness: Mihaly Biro (tr). **United States Holocaust Memorial Museum:** Courtesy of Adalbert Feher (cr). **113** Eszter Hargittai: (bl). Beth Hatefutsoth, Photo Archive, Tel Aviv: Yad Vashem Photo Archive,Jerusalem (tl). Hungarian National Museum, Historical Photographic Collection: (tr). **United States Holocaust Memorial Museum:** Courtesy of Magyar Nemzeti Muzeum Torteneti Fenykeptar (br). **114-115** Getty Images: George Hales/Fox Photos. **116** Express Newspapers: Strube (bl). **United States Holocaust Memorial Museum:** Courtesy of Oesterreichische Gesellschaft fuer Zeitgeschichte (t). **117** akg-images: Bildarchiv Pisarek (tr). **Corbis:** Bettmann (cl). **United States Holocaust Memorial Museum:** Courtesy of Dwight D. Eisenhower Library (b). **118** New York Times: (b). United States Holocaust Memorial Museum: Courtesy of Milton Koch (tr). The David S. Wyman Institute for Holocaust Studies Washington D.C: (cl). **119** Bildarchiv Preußischer Kulturbesitz, Berlin: (tl). Government Press Office: Fritz Cohen (tr). **United States Holocaust Memorial Museum:** Courtesy of Musée de la Resistance et de la Deportation (br); Courtesy of Beit Hannah Senesh (cl). Courtesy of photo archive, Yad Vashem: (b). **120** Corbis: Bettmann (bl). Wiener Library: (br). **121** United States Holocaust Memorial Museum: Courtesy of Sigmund Baum (tr); Courtesy of Frihedsmuseet (tl); Jewish Historical Museum of Yugoslavia (bl); Courtesy of Gavra Mandil (br). **124** United States Holocaust Memorial Museum: Courtesy of Mert Bland (cl); Courtesy of Hiroki Sugihara (bc); Courtesy of Thomas Veres, Photo by Thomas Veres (br). **124-125** Courtesy of photo archive, Yad Vashem: Yad Vashem Artifacts Collection. Gift of the Pacifici family, Italy (t). **125** Getty Images: Hulton Archive (cr). **United States Holocaust Memorial Museum:** Leopold Page Photograph Collection (bl). Courtesy of photo archive, Yad Vashem: (tr). **126-127** United States Holocaust Memorial Museum: Courtesy of Bep Meyer Zion. **130** Bavarian State Library, Munich: (t). Courtesy of photo archive, Yad Vashem: (b). **131** akg-images: (tr) (br). United States Holocaust Memorial Museum: Courtesy of Hanna Meyer-Moses (tc); Courtesy of Beatrice Muchman (tl). **132** American Jewish Archives: (l). Corbis: Bettmann (t). Science Photo Library: Volker Steger (br). **133** British Pathé Ltd: (br). Corbis: Bettmann (t). United States Holocaust Memorial Museum: Courtesy of National Archives and Records Administration, College Park (c). **134** akg-images: (bl): © Alexandra Szyk Bracie (tl). **134-135** © Beit Lohamei Haghetaot/The Ghetto Fighters House Museum: family of Jacob Davidson. **135** © Beit Lohamei Haghetaot/The Ghetto Fighters House Museum: (cra); family of Jacob Davidson (br). United States Holocaust Memorial Museum: (cr). Courtesy of photo archive, Yad Vashem: (tc). **136** © Alexandre Oler: as published in Witness, Images of Auschwitz with illustrations by David Olère and text by Alexandre Oler, 1998 WESTWIND PRESS. **137** akg-images: (c). Florida Center for Instructional Technology: (t). United States Holocaust Memorial Museum: (bl). Courtesy of photo archive, Yad Vashem: (br). **138-139** United States Holocaust Memorial Museum: Courtesy of National Archives and Records Administration, College Park (c). **140** Imperial War Museum: (cr). TopFoto: (tl). United States Holocaust Memorial Museum: Courtesy of Archiwum Panstwowego Muzeum na Majdanku (c). **141** akg-images: Benno Gantner (bl); Ullstein Bild (t). Corbis: (r). United States Holocaust Memorial Museum: Courtesy of Albert Abramson (tr); Courtesy of Seymour Schenkman (bc). **144** akg-images. **145** akg-images: (tl) (br). (c) Canadian War Museum (CWM): (cr). Collection of the Yad Vashem Art Museum, Jerusalem: Zinovii Tolkatchev (1903-1977) A Mother and her Baby, Auschwitz, 1945 Pencil on paper. Gift of Anel Tolkatcheva and Ilya Tolkatchev, Kiev (bl). **146-147** Getty Images: Hulton Archive. **150** akg-images: (tr) (br). United States Holocaust Memorial Museum: Courtesy of Dr. Robert G. Waits (c). Courtesy of photo archive, Yad Vashem: (bl). **151** akg-images: Ullstein Bild (bl). Corbis: Bettmann (br); Hulton-Deutsch Collection (t). **152** Collection of the Yad Vashem Art Museum, Jerusalem: Yad Vashem Art Museum, Gift of Sigmund A. Rolat, New York, in loving memory of his parents, Henryk ans Mania, who perished in the Holocaust (cr). **153** United States Holocaust Memorial Museum: (cl); Courtesy of George Kadish/Zvi Kadushin (cr); Courtesy of Leah Lahav (tr); Courtesy of Ruchana Medine White (b). **154** United States Holocaust Memorial Museum: Courtesy of George Kadish/Zvi Kadushin (bl); Courtesy of Alice Lev (tr); Courtesy of Regina Gutman Speigel (tl). **154-155** United States Holocaust Memorial Museum: Courtesy of Chaia Libstug-Rosenblum (b). **155** United States Holocaust Memorial Museum: Courtesy of Inge Berner (tr); Courtesy of George Kadish/Zvi Kadushin (tl); Courtesy of Diane Popowski (br); Courtesy of Yivo Institute for Jewish Research (tc). **156**

Photo courtesy of HIAS Archives: (tl). United States Holocaust Memorial Museum: Courtesy of Schaja and Pnina Klein (bl); Courtesy of Bernard Marks (c). **157** Getty Images: AFP (t); Time Life Pictures (bl). **United States Holocaust Memorial Museum:** Courtesy of Elinor Gabriel (br). **160-161** Corbis: Michael St. Maur Sheil. **162** Czech Memorial Scrolls Trust: (cl). Getty Images: (c); Olympic Museum/Allsport (tr). **United States Holocaust Memorial Museum:** Courtesy of Hadassah Bimko Rosensaft (b). **163** Getty Images: Ralph Orlowski (bl). Angela Gluck Wood: (br). © Beit Lohamei Haghetaot/The Ghetto Fighters House Museum: (tl). **Central Zionist Archives, Jerusalem:** (b). John C. Menszer: (cr). **165** Corbis: Henny Ray Abrams/Reuters (br). Tamara Deuel: (tl). **United States Holocaust Memorial Museum:** Courtesy of Lilo Plaschkes (bl). **Collection of the Yad Vashem Art Museum, Jerusalem:** Yehuda Bacon (b.1929) In Memory of the Czech Transport to the Gas Chambers, 1945. Charcoal on paper. Loan of the artist (tr). **168** Alamy Images: Popperfoto (bl). Getty Images: Time Life Pictures (t). **United States Holocaust Memorial Museum:** Courtesy of National Archives and Records Administration, College Park (br). **169** Corbis: Bettmann (t). Getty Images: Gjon Mili/Time & Life Pictures (br). Le Monde: Plantu (br). **172** Corbis: Bettmann (bl). United States Holocaust Memorial Museum: Courtesy of National Archives and Records Administration, College Park (br). **172-173** akg-images: Licensed by DACS, 2007 (tc). **173** Corbis: Bettmann (br). Getty Images: Timothy Clary/AFP (tr). **United States Holocaust Memorial Museum:** Corbis-Bettmann (cr); Courtesy of Benjamin Ferencz (bl). **174** Angela Gluck Wood: (t) (br). **175** akg-images: Ullstein Bild (br). Getty Images: Piotr Malecki (bl). Angela Gluck Wood: (t). Stan Kujawa: Photographersdirect.com (tr). **176** Corbis: Reuters (r). Angela Gluck Wood: (cl). **176-177** Corbis: Fabrizio Bensch/Pool/EPA (b). **177** Alamy Images: pbpgalleries (tr). Holocaust Resource Center - Temple Judea of Manhasset: (br). Dina Koren: Photographersdirect.com (tl). **182** Empics Ltd: Adam Butler/AP (br); Diether Endlicher/AP (bl); Mark Gilliland/AP (t). **183** Action Reconciliation Service for Peace, Berlin: David Grodzki (cl). Empics Ltd: Elaine Thompson/AP (tr). Angela Gluck Wood: (cr). Collection of the Yad Vashem Art Museum, Jerusalem: Petr Ginz (1928-1944) Moon Landscape, 1942-1944 Pencil on paper. Gift of Otto Ginz, Haifa (b). **184-185** akg-images: Juergen Sorges.

Jacket images: *Front.* **PunchStock:** Stockbyte Platinum

All other images © Dorling Kindersley
For further information see: www.dkimages.com

Jacket images: *Front.* **PunchStock:** Stockbyte Platinum

All other images © Dorling Kindersley
For further information see: www.dkimages.com

Thanks to Constance Novis for proofreading and to Hilary Bird for indexing.

With thanks to the following people from the USC Shoah Foundation Institute: Douglas Greenberg, Professor of History and Executive Director, Karen Jungblut, Director, Archival Access & Special Projects, Kim Simon, Director, Partnerships & International Programs

Thanks also to the following people whose testimonies are featured in this book: Alexander Van Kollem, Aniela Ania Radek, Bernard Schuster, Claire Boren, Demetrius Dvoichenko-Markov, Diana Golden, Emma Mogilensky, Eric Richmond, Felicia Carmelly, Fred Baer, Fred Spiegel, Henry Greenblatt, Henry Oster, Jacob Sandbrand, Julia Lentini, Leon Bass, Leonie Hilton, Lola Putt, Mayer Schondorf, Michelle Cohen-Rodriguez, Peter Hersch, Peter Less, Renée Firestone, Rose Silberberg-Skier, Ruth Gruber, Sigi Hart, Thea Rumstein, Vera Eden, Vera Gissing, William Williams

The publisher wishes to acknowledge the following publications. Every effort has been made to contact the rights owners in each case but the publisher would welcome information on any omissions.

p18 *The Promised Land*, by Mary Antin (Penguin Books); p19 Adapted and abridged from *Chasing Shadows*, by Hugo Gryn with Naomi Gryn (Penguin Books) and from the documentary film *The Sabbath Bride*; p38 *The Holocaust, The Jewish Tragedy* by Sir Martin Gilbert (Harper Collins); p49 *Kristallnacht at the Dinslaken Orphanage* by YS Herz (Yad Vashem Studies, XI, 1976); p93 *Commandant of Auschwitz* by Rudolf Hoess (Wiedenfeld and Nicholson, a division of the Orion Publishing Group); p110 *If this is a Man*, by Primo Levi (Random House/Einaudi); p128 *The Diary of a Young Girl: The Definitive Edition*, by Anne Frank (Penguin Books/Random House); p129 *Salvaged Pages: Young Writer Diaries of the Holocaust*, edited by Alexandra Zapruder (Yale University Press). The publisher also wishes to acknowledge Sir Gilbert Martin whose maps were an inspiration during the production of this book.

CREDITS AND ACKNOWLEDGEMENTS